Contents

W9-AZS-729

©2005 by Evan-Moor Corp. • Daily Summer Activities 3-4 • EMC 1030

How to Use *Daily Summer Activities*

Provide Time

Make sure that your child has a quiet time for practice. The practice session should be short and successful. Consider your child's personality and other activities as you decide how to schedule daily practice periods.

Provide Materials

Your child will need a quiet place to work. Put extra writing and drawing paper, scissors, crayons, pencils, and a glue stick in a tub or box. Store the supplies and *Daily Summer Activities* in the work area you and your child choose.

Provide Encouragement and Support

Your response is important to your child's feelings of success. Keep your remarks positive. Recognize the effort your child has made. Correct mistakes together. Work toward independence, guiding practice when necessary.

Track Progress

Each weekly section begins with a record form. Use the form to track progress. Have your child color the symbols as each day's work is completed.

What's in *Daily Summer Activities?*

Ten Weekly Sections

Each of the ten weekly sections provides basic skill practice in several subject areas. The practice sessions are short, giving your child a review of what was learned during the previous school year.

Weekly Record Form

In addition to providing a means to record work completed, the record form also contains:

— a reading log where your child records the number of minutes read each day (See pages 4 and 5 for reading suggestions.)

— a weekly spelling list

— a place where your child can record interesting daily events

Reading

Your child will read two short stories, one fiction and one nonfiction, each week and then answer questions to show comprehension. Have your child read a story aloud for additional practice. Encourage your child to attempt words that are unfamiliar, but do offer help if your child appears frustrated. For example, you might ask, "What word that begins with *p* might make sense in this sentence?" or "You know that this part of the word says *and*. Can you add the rest of the word?"

Language Skills

Your child will practice punctuation, capitalization, and grammar, as well as phonetic and word attack skills.

Math

Computation, word problems, and other appropriate math concepts are practiced each day.

Spelling

Each weekly record form includes a list of ten spelling words to learn. Have your child practice the spelling words in several ways: copy them several times, write them from memory, and spell them aloud. On Friday, ask your child to spell the week's words. This testing may be done orally or in writing. Add any missed words to the next week's spelling list for additional practice. A compiled spelling list can be found on the inside back cover.

Handwriting

Your child will write sentences, poems, and lists, using good handwriting.

Geography

This weekly activity will provide practice reading the symbols used on maps and using maps to locate information.

Writing

A creative writing experience is included each week.

Encourage Reading

Be a Model

The most important thing you can do for your child is to read. Even though your child is now an independent reader, you should still share books by reading to and with your child. It is important that your child see you reading. Read books, magazines, and newspapers. Read signs, labels, letters, directions, and displays as well. Visit libraries and bookstores and don't forget to read your way through museums, parks, stores, and playgrounds.

Helping Your Child Select Appropriate Books

Choosing a book that your child wants to read and that is appropriate for independent reading can be difficult. You can assist in several ways:

- Help your child become familiar with the organization of the library or bookstore. Know how to use the computer search tools to find the titles of books on a specific topic and locate individual books.

- Teach your child to use the "five finger" method to test readability.

The Five Finger Method

1. Your child selects a page near the beginning of the book.

2. Your child reads the page, raising a finger for each word that he or she doesn't know. (Proper nouns do not count.) If no fingers are raised when the page is finished, the book may be too easy. If all five fingers are raised before the end of the page, the book is probably too difficult for independent reading.

3. Your child selects two other pages (one in the middle of the book and one at the end) and repeats the process.

4. Using this trial reading, your child decides whether the book is a good choice. If the book seems too difficult, but he or she really wants to read it, help him or her decide on a strategy:

- Read the book together.

- Have an adult available to help with hard words and ideas.

©2005 by Evan-Moor Corp. • Daily Summer Activities 3-4 • EMC 1030

Books to Read

At this age, your child can read many different kinds of books. He or she may have found a favorite series and reads only books from that series. Don't worry! There is nothing wrong with enjoying a particular style or character. This list suggests only a few of the wonderful chapter books that you will find in your library and bookstore.

The Boy Who Ate Dog Biscuits by Betsy Sachs; Random House, 1989.

Charlotte's Web by E. B. White; HarperTrophy, 1999.

Comeback! Four True Stories by Jim O'Connor; Random House, 1992.

Ducks in Danger by Emily Costello; Camelot, 1999.

Emily Arrow Promises to Do Better This Year by Patricia Reilly Giff; Yearling Books, 1990.

Encyclopedia Brown Saves the Day by Donald J. Sobol; Bantam Skylark, 1982.

First Books—Biographies; Franklin Watts, Inc.

Freckle Juice by Judy Blume; Yearling Books, 1978.

Harriet the Spy by Louise Fitzhugh; HarperTrophy, 1990.

How to Eat Fried Worms by Thomas Rockwell; Franklin Watts, 1973.

Junie B. Jones and the Stupid Smelly Bus by Barbara Park; Random Library, 1992.

Little House on the Prairie by Laura Ingalls Wilder; HarperTrophy, 1973.

The Littles by John Peterson; Scholastic, 1993.

Ramona's World by Beverly Cleary; Morrow Junior, 1999.

Rookie Biographies by Carol Greene; Childrens Press.

Sarah, Plain and Tall by Patricia MacLachlan; HarperTrophy, 1987.

Sideways Stories from Wayside School by Louis Sachar; Avon, 1998.

Skinnybones by Barbara Park; Bullseye Books, 1997.

Starting School by Johanna Hurwitz; Morrow Junior, 1998.

Stuart Little by E. B. White; HarperCollins, 1974.

Tales of a Fourth Grade Nothing by Judy Blume; E.P. Dutton, 1972.

The Water Horse by Dick King-Smith; Crown Publishing, 1998.

The Whipping Boy by Sid Fleischman; Troll, 1989.

Learning Excursions

Learning takes place everywhere. Here is a list of places to go, things to do, and ways to build "learning power" over the summer.

1. Go to the public library every week. Choose some "read aloud" books together. Allow your child to choose some books independently. Check out books for yourself.

2. Visit local museums and historic sites. Pick up a guide to points of interest in your area. The Chamber of Commerce and AAA are good sources for this material. Pack a picnic and spend the day learning and having fun.

3. Collect some art materials and work together to create a collage, a mobile, or other artwork. Get the whole family involved.

4. Keep a family journal in a spiral notebook or other blank book. Write a topic at the top of each page. Ask each family member to make an entry every day over the summer. Here are some journal topics to get you started:
   • Is it most important to be happy, good, or successful? Why?
   • If you could meet one person from long ago, who would it be? Why?
   • Describe your ideal vacation.

5. Plant a garden. If you are short on space, plant in containers.

6. Find a theatrical event at a local theater that is appropriate for the whole family.

7. Go to a concert or listen to a new classical composer each week.

8. Create a movie. Make a video tape of your favorite story. Create a simple script and costumes. Practice until everyone is comfortable, then shoot!

9. Build vocabulary power. Play word games such as Scrabble®, Pictionary®, Balderdash®, Scattergories®, and Boggle®.

10. Build muscle power. Go for a hike. Begin with easy walks and work up to longer hikes.

11. Build memory power. Play "Going to Grandmother's House." The first player says, "I'm going to Grandmother's house, and I'm going to take a pizza." The next player says, "I'm going to Grandmother's house, and I'm going to take a pizza and flowers." Each player must repeat, in exact order, the items named in the previous rounds, and then add something. Play until only one person can list all items.

12. Build reasoning power. While traveling in the car or waiting in a restaurant, play "Twenty Questions." One person thinks of an object. Players take turns asking questions that can be answered with a "yes" or "no." It is helpful to ask questions that eliminate broad categories, instead of making random guesses. Guide children toward questions such as "Would it fit in a shoebox?" "Is it useful?" "Is it made of metal?" If the object is not named after twenty questions, it must be revealed.

©2005 by Evan-Moor Corp. • Daily Summer Activities 3-4 • EMC 1030

Cursive Handwriting

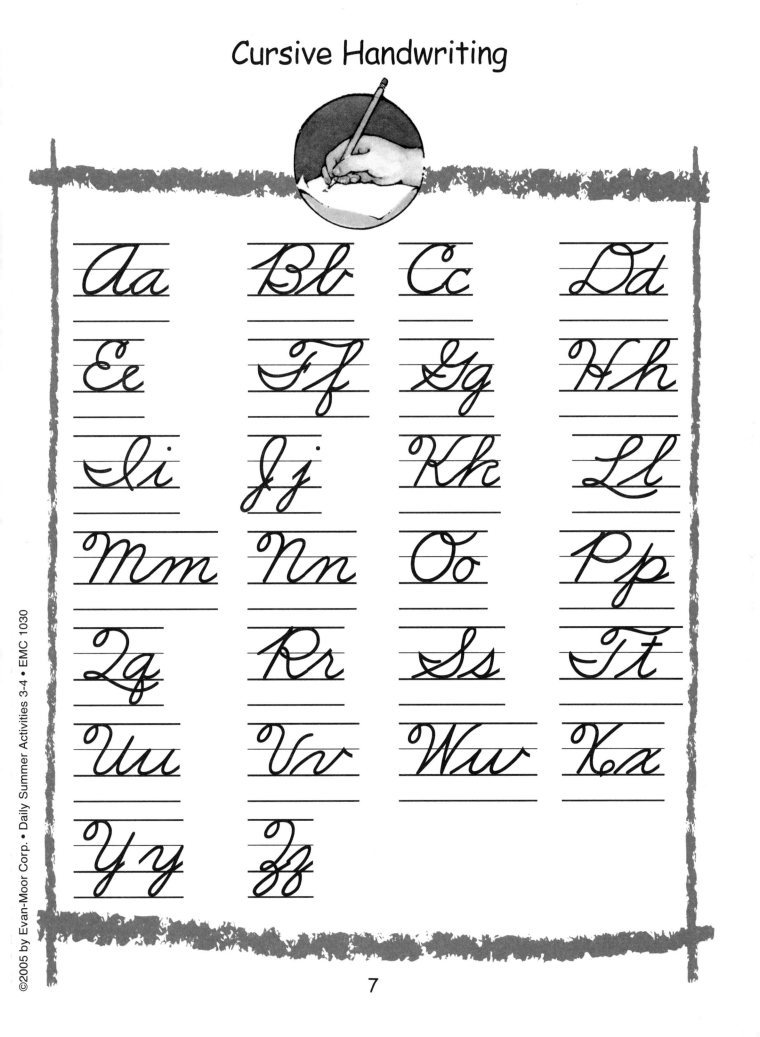

Aa Bb Cc Dd

Ee Ff Gg Hh

Ii Jj Kk Ll

Mm Nn Oo Pp

Qq Rr Ss Tt

Uu Vv Ww Xx

Yy Zz

Color a ⭐ for each page finished.

Parent's Initials

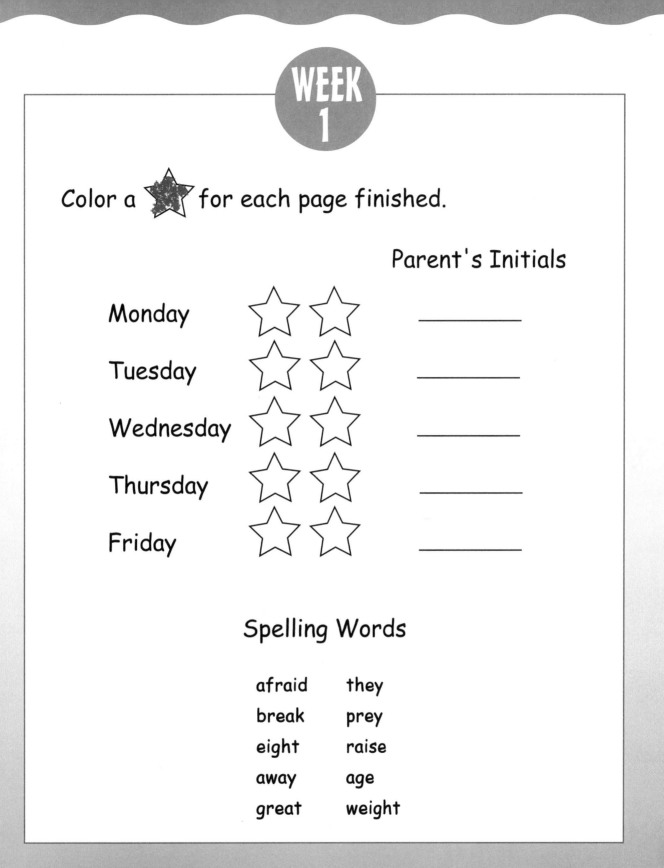

		Parent's Initials
Monday	☆ ☆	_____
Tuesday	☆ ☆	_____
Wednesday	☆ ☆	_____
Thursday	☆ ☆	_____
Friday	☆ ☆	_____

Spelling Words

afraid	they
break	prey
eight	raise
away	age
great	weight

A Memorable Moment What sticks in your mind about this week? Write about it.

_____

_____

_____

_____

_____

_____

Keeping Track Color a book for every 15 minutes you read.

Monday	Tuesday	Wednesday	Thursday	Friday

Describe a character you read about this week.

_____

_____

_____

_____

_____

_____

An Unnamed Story

Rachel shoved her navy blue sweatshirt into her bulging duffel bag and zipped the zipper. She had been packing and repacking for a week. Now she felt sure that everything was ready. She carried her duffel and sleeping bags out to the car, threw them into the backseat, and climbed in. Her mother started the car and smiled in the rearview mirror.

"All set?"

Rachel nodded, trying to smile in return. She couldn't understand what was happening to her. She did not like the odd fluttering that was tickling her tummy.

"Am I coming down with the flu?" Rachel thought to herself. "It would be awful to be sick at camp."

Rachel had been counting the days since school let out. She was eager for this moment to arrive. But now that it was here and she was actually heading for Camp Wapiti, Rachel's feelings were not quite so clear.

1. Circle the best title for the story.

    a. Rachel Gets Sick   c. Rachel and Her Mother

    b. Rachel Goes to Camp   d. Camp Wapiti

2. Name at least three other things that might be in Rachel's bag.

_____

3. What was the cause of the strange feeling in Rachel's stomach?

_____

4. Why do you think Rachel wasn't sure about going to camp?

_____

_____

1. mr and mrs washington are planning to go to australia this summer

_____

_____

2. here spot shouted kevin as he ran toward cindys house

_____

_____

3. seventeen anteaters marched across peru singing yankee doodle dandy

_____

_____

MATH TIME

Try to work these problems in a minute or less.

6 + 3	5 + 5	9 − 2	15 − 8	2 + 8	7 + 6	6 + 8	4 + 9
8 + 5	14 − 5	16 − 9	6 + 4	7 + 8	9 + 6	10 − 3	13 − 6
7 + 7	6 + 9	8 + 8	12 − 6	6 + 6	5 + 6	15 − 7	8 + 7

©2005 by Evan-Moor Corp. • Daily Summer Activities 3-4 • EMC 1030

Spell It!

Read your spelling words aloud. Circle the letters that are used to make the long a sound in each word.

afraid	they	break	prey	eight
raise	away	age	great	weight

Brainstorm with your family to make a list of more words that have the long a sound. Use extra paper if needed.

Fill in each blank in the poem using one of your spelling words.
Then copy the poem on the lines below using your best handwriting.
(Hint: One of the words is used twice!)

The _____ of _____
Is amazingly _____.
The _____ of nine
Is tremendously fine.

Language Bytes

Nouns are words that name people, places, and things. Write each noun in the list below under the correct heading. Then add one more noun to each group.

People	Places	Things
_____	_____	_____
_____	_____	_____
_____	_____	_____
_____	_____	_____
_____	_____	_____

bank   peanut butter   restaurant   raccoon

shoe   firefighter   Susan   baby

encyclopedia   parent   park   Disneyland

MATH TIME

Find the answers.

```
  8      7      4      9      1      5      5      4      7
  2      8      5      0      6      3      8      7      9
+ 1    + 8    + 6    + 9    + 5    + 7    + 3    + 2    + 9


  9      6      5      4      9      7      7      9      5
  4      3      1      7      5      9      5      6      4
+ 8    + 7    + 6    + 6    + 7    + 8    + 6    + 4    + 5
```

©2005 by Evan-Moor Corp. • Daily Summer Activities 3-4 • EMC 1030

Florence Nightingale

Florence Nightingale was born in Florence, Italy, in the year 1820. Her family was very wealthy. They lived in a beautiful home and had many friends.

As Florence grew up, she learned Greek and Latin and mathematics. She also learned to be a good hostess and to run a large household. But Florence liked studying more than she liked giving parties. She wanted to help others, especially those who were sick or suffering.

Florence learned to be a nurse by working in hospitals in France and Germany. She was a very good nurse, and at the age of thirty-three, she was placed in charge of a hospital in London.

The next year, Florence was sent to Eastern Europe, where English soldiers were involved in a war. Florence took thirty-eight other nurses with her. They had little in the way of supplies or medicines. But Florence worked hard to help the wounded and became famous for her efforts.

Today the name Florence Nightingale is known around the world as a symbol of help to those in need.

1. In the first paragraph, what is the meaning of the word *wealthy*?

   _____

2. Florence wanted to help others.   True   False

3. Florence traveled to _____ to learn to be a nurse.

       Spain and England   Russia and Sweden   France and Germany

4. Florence Nightingale is remembered today because

   _____ .

Language Bytes

Homophones are words that sound the same but have different meanings. Fill in the blanks in each pair of sentences using a pair of homophones from the box.

1. Mallory _____ a strange noise.

   The _____ of elephants stopped at the water hole.

2. Aunt Sue made pancakes with whole wheat _____.

   There is only one red _____ in the garden.

3. Alonzo paid his subway _____ with quarters.

   Maria is planning to show her lamb at the county _____.

4. After the hike, Sharon had a blister on her _____.

   Mike's broken arm is beginning to _____.

5. Make up a pair of sentences to go with the pair of homophones you did not use.

   _____

   _____

| flower |
| flour |
| fare |
| fair |
| heal |
| heel |
| heard |
| herd |
| weak |
| week |

MATH⏱TIME **Find the answers.**

68	77	53	28	64	92	32
+ 21	- 33	+ 25	+ 40	- 52	+ 7	+ 57

49	34	87	72	56	21	40
- 17	+ 54	- 76	+ 25	+ 43	+ 66	+ 28

©2005 by Evan-Moor Corp. • Daily Summer Activities 3-4 • EMC 1030

Geography

Use an atlas or a globe.

Find the continent of North America.
Color it red.

Write an X on South America.

Color Africa green.

Label the Pacific Ocean and the
Atlantic Ocean.

Color all the oceans blue.

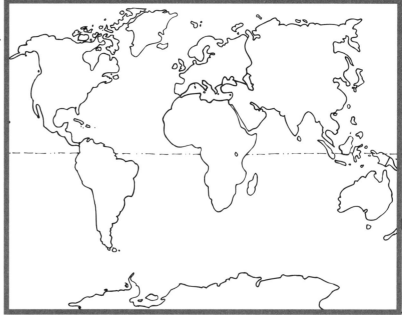

Write a List

Make a list of four fun things to do on Saturdays.

1. _____

2. _____

3. _____

4. _____

Write a sentence or two telling which of these things you like best and why.

_____

_____

_____

MATH⏱TIME

483	277	648	920	335	583
+ 111	- 204	- 435	+ 67	- 132	+ 416

756	269	124	356	888	794
- 133	+ 420	- 103	+ 643	- 575	+ 205

Language Bytes

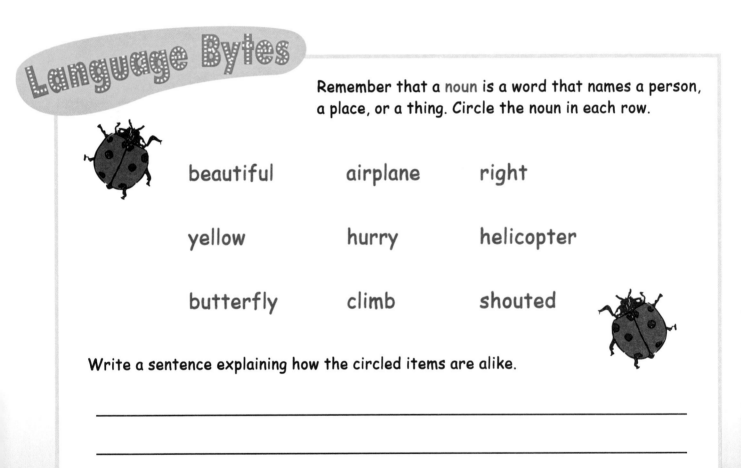

Remember that a noun is a word that names a person, a place, or a thing. Circle the noun in each row.

beautiful	airplane	right
yellow	hurry	helicopter
butterfly	climb	shouted

Write a sentence explaining how the circled items are alike.

_____

_____

_____

18

Week 1

Thursday

Write the name of each fruit on the line next to its picture.

Write your list again, this time in alphabetical order.

_____   _____

_____   _____

_____   _____

_____   _____

_____   _____

Find the answers.

1. Shirley collected seashells on her vacation at the seashore. On Sunday, she found 3 conch shells. On Monday, she found 7 olive shells. On Tuesday, she found 9 scallop shells. On Wednesday, she found 8 whelk shells. How many seashells did Shirley find altogether?

_____

2. Fred earned $9.75 washing cars. He decided to spend some of the money on a movie ticket. If the movie ticket cost $3.50, how much money did Fred have left?

_____

3. Sandy has already finished reading two books on her summer reading list. The first book had 211 pages. The second book had 168 pages. How many pages has Sandy read altogether?

_____

Friday

Week 1

Who's Behind the Door?

If you knocked on each of these doors, who would answer? Draw a line from each door to the character that would most likely answer your knock.

What would each character say? Write a response for each character in the speech bubble.

©2005 by Evan-Moor Corp. • Daily Summer Activities 3-4 • EMC 1030

Color a 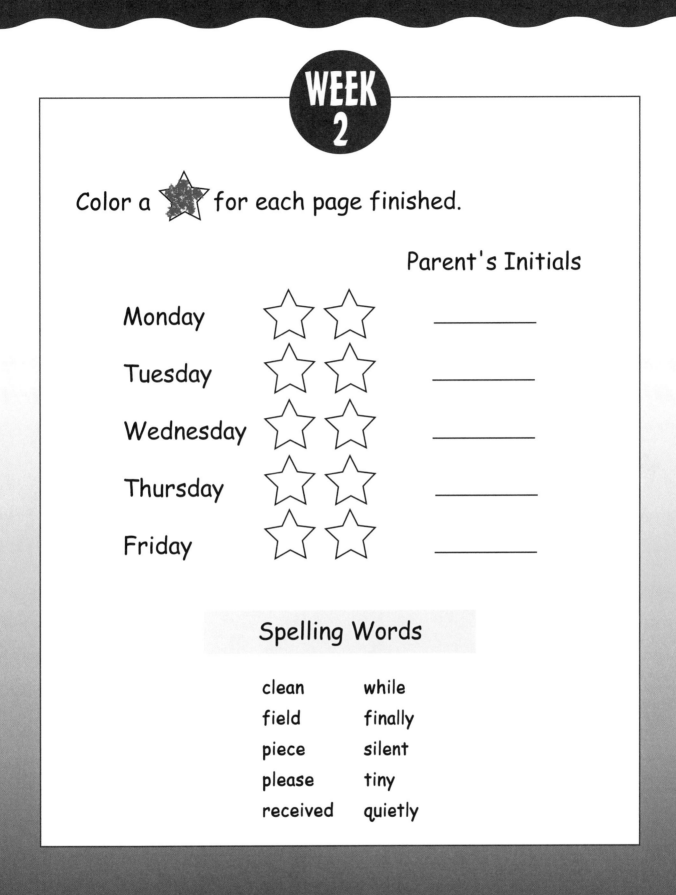 for each page finished.

Parent's Initials

Monday ☆☆ _____

Tuesday ☆☆ _____

Wednesday ☆☆ _____

Thursday ☆☆ _____

Friday ☆☆ _____

Spelling Words

clean	while
field	finally
piece	silent
please	tiny
received	quietly

A Memorable Moment What sticks in your mind about this week? Write about it.

_____

_____

_____

_____

_____

_____

_____

Keeping Track Color a book for every 15 minutes you read.

Monday	Tuesday	Wednesday	Thursday	Friday

Describe the setting of a story you read this week.

_____

_____

_____

_____

_____

_____

Please Make Sense

Find the nonsense word in each pair of sentences below. Replace that word in each sentence with the same real word. Make sure the word you choose makes sense in both of the sentences.

The carpenter uses a hammer to tumple the nails.

My mother bought a tumple of sugar.

_____

The coach told us to stand in a straight wingding.

Mr. Hoover used clean paper to wingding the shelves.

_____

It is hard to be lammy when you are waiting for your turn.

The lammy in the hospital bed was feeling much better.

_____

Elliott threw a doodop to Beau, who then made a touchdown.

I hope that I doodop my math test.

_____

The neighbor's dog likes to gullybug all night.

The gullybug on a birch tree is smooth and white.

_____

Dad said, "Please use your puffit instead of your fingers."

When we came to the puffit in the road, we were not
sure which way to go.

_____

Annie likes to keevil her baby sister to sleep.

Mark and his friend climbed to the top of a large keevil.

_____

©2005 by Evan-Moor Corp. • Daily Summer Activities 3-4 • EMC 1030

Write It Right

1. my fathers office is at 201 elmwood dr frankfort kentucky

_____

_____

2. where is the baseball field at

_____

3. paul and janet has invited us over to there house

_____

_____

MATH TIME

Find the answers.

3	5	6	5	7	9	7
x 4	x 2	x 2	x 4	x 8	x 3	x 2

5	3	4	9	5	6	6
x 8	x 7	x 6	x 4	x 7	x 8	x 3

9	4	3	8	7	5	9
x 9	x 7	x 8	x 8	x 9	x 5	x 2

©2005 by Evan-Moor Corp. • Daily Summer Activities 3-4 • EMC 1030

Spell It!

Answer these questions using your spelling words.

1. Which word means "very, very small"? _____

2. Which word means "an open, grassy area"? _____

3. What is the opposite of *dirty*? _____

4. What do you call one part of a puzzle, or one slice of a pie? _____

5. Which word means "at last"? _____

6. Which word do you use when you are asking someone to give you something?

    _____

7. What is the opposite of *sent*? _____

Fill in the blanks in the sentences below using your spelling words.
Then copy the sentences using your best handwriting.

_____ the giant slept.

Jack crept _____ out of the cupboard.

He tried to be _____.

_____

_____

_____

_____

_____

These sentences are part of a familiar story. What is the name of the story?

_____

Language Bytes

Plurals are nouns that mean "more than one." Match each noun on the left to its plural on the right.

child	bananas
tree	geese
goose	girls
class	children
leaf	trees
banana	classes
boy	leaves
girl	boys

Notice that plurals are formed in several different ways. Which way of forming plurals is used most often?

_____

MATH⊙TIME

Find the answers.

9 x 8	6 x 7	8 x 8	6 x 6	5 x 9	8 x 4	9 x 2
6 x 5	8 x 7	5 x 3	3 x 8	7 x 7	6 x 3	5 x 4
3 x 4	6 x 9	7 x 2	4 x 4	7 x 6	8 x 2	9 x 4

26

Week 2

Tuesday

©2005 by Evan-Moor Corp. • Daily Summer Activities 3–4 • EMC 1030

A Wonder of the Sea

The octopus is an odd-looking animal that lives in the ocean. It has a soft body that is covered with a tough membrane called a *mantle*. It has eight long arms called *tentacles*. The tentacles are lined with strong muscles that act like suction cups. The octopus uses these tentacles to crack open the shells of clams and crabs. It then uses its sharp beak to eat the meat of the shellfish.

The octopus has a very interesting and unusual body. It has large bright eyes that can see quite well. It has three hearts. Like fish, it uses gills to breathe underwater. The octopus moves by drawing water into its body and then quickly forcing the water out. This force propels the octopus backward through the water. The octopus can shoot an inky liquid out of its body. This liquid forms a cloud in the water and helps hide the octopus from sharks and other animals that might try to eat it. The octopus can also hide by changing colors to blend with its surroundings. When the octopus is excited, it can turn bright colors such as red, purple, or blue.

Octopuses come in many sizes. The smallest octopuses are only a few inches across. The largest may reach nearly 30 feet when measured across its outstretched tentacles. The octopus may look scary, but it rarely attacks people.

The octopus is truly one of the wonders of the sea.

1. What are tentacles? _____

2. What is a mantle? _____

3. What does the octopus eat? _____

4. List two ways the octopus can hide from danger. _____

_____

5. Why does the author call the octopus a "wonder of the sea"?

_____

Wednesday

Week 2

©2005 by Evan-Moor Corp. • Daily Summer Activities 3-4 • EMC 1030

Language Bytes

Write the plural of each word in the blank. You will need to make spelling changes in some of the words.

1. Sarah could not find her car _____.
   key

2. The _____ gathered for a neighborhood party.
   family

3. Seven _____ danced around the fire.
   elf

4. The waiter served six _____ of ice water.
   glass

5. The _____ had fun at the circus.
   child

6. Mrs. Soldowski has four _____.
   rabbit

MATH TIME

Find the answers.

36	94	57	66	75	63	94
+ 29	+ 48	- 34	+ 91	- 25	+ 38	- 73

84	69	78	32	43	88	65
+ 58	- 42	+ 88	+ 59	+ 64	- 54	- 21

©2005 by Evan-Moor Corp. • Daily Summer Activities 3-4 • EMC 1030

Geography

Use an atlas, a globe, or a map of the United States to find the name of each numbered body of water.

1. _____

2. _____

3. _____

4. _____

5. _____

6. _____

7. _____

8. _____

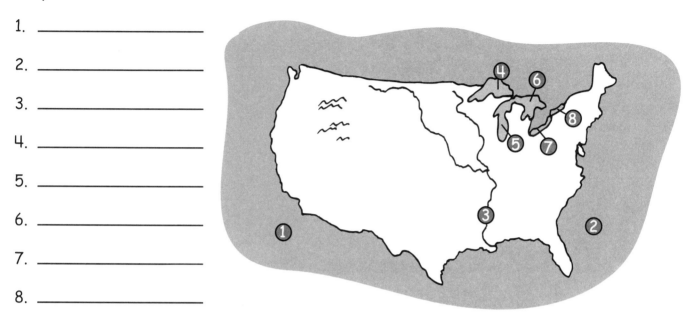

In My Own Words

Read the paragraph below and then write a topic sentence that could begin the paragraph.

_____

_____

_____

Mr. and Mrs. Smith play tennis or golf almost every day. Buddy Smith is on the football team at the high school. Sissy Smith is a star forward on the soccer team at the park. The Smiths all enjoy swimming and running on the weekends.

MATH TIME

$30 \div 5 =$ $16 \div 4 =$ $27 \div 3 =$ $24 \div 6 =$

$10 \div 2 =$ $18 \div 3 =$ $35 \div 7 =$ $25 \div 5 =$

$12 \div 3 =$ $36 \div 6 =$ $40 \div 5 =$ $32 \div 4 =$

Language Bytes

Complete these analogies.

1. Quack is to duck as bark is to _____.

2. Shoe is to foot as hat is to _____.

3. Red is to stop as green is to _____.

4. Happy is to sad as up is to _____.

5. Feather is to bird as scale is to _____.

6 Cocker spaniel is to dog as apple is to _____.

Language Bytes

Synonyms are words that mean the same thing. Write a synonym for the underlined word in each sentence.

1. My grandmother has a <u>little</u> dog named Toby. _____

2. I had a <u>terrible</u> headache yesterday. _____

3. Lynne was <u>glad</u> to see her friend. _____

MATH TIME

Find the answers.

1. Mary Lou has a fish tank. She has 3 of each kind of fish in her tank. She has swordtails, guppies, and angelfish. How many fish does Mary Lou have in her tank? You may want to draw a picture to help solve the problem. _____

2. Angie wants to give 4 carrots to each of her 5 horses. How many carrots does she need? _____

3. Make up a word problem using a multiplication fact. Give it to someone to solve.

_____

_____

_____

Two boys, Kirt and Andrew, and three girls, Doris, Gail, and Barbara, went out to dinner. Each one in the group ordered a different meal. Read the clues below to find out where each person sat and what each had for dinner. Write your answers on the lines.

Doris sat between Gail and the boy who had a burrito.

The girl who had pizza was not Barbara.

Andrew sat next to the girl who had fried chicken.

The girl who had fried chicken sat in chair #4.

The boy who had spaghetti sat between Barbara and Kirt.

Gail had a hamburger.

Kirt sat in chair #1.

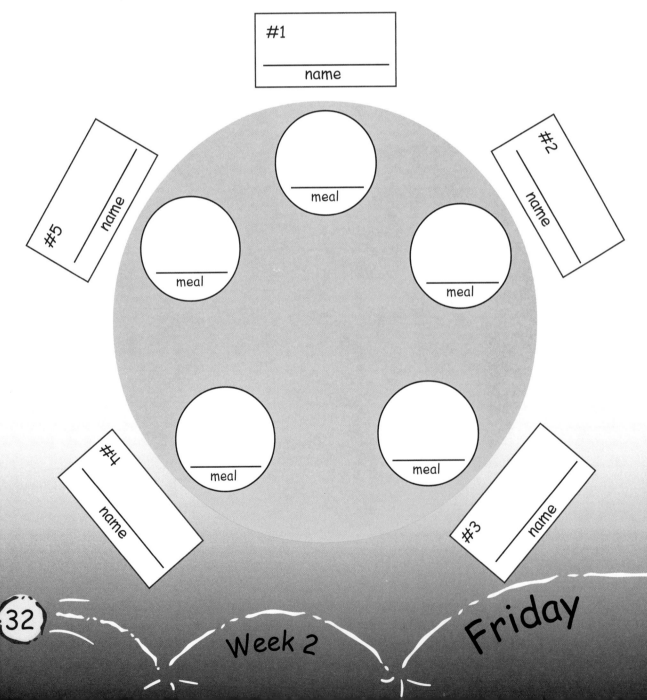

#1

name

#2

name

#5

name

meal

meal

meal

meal

meal

#4

name

#3

name

©2005 by Evan-Moor Corp. • Daily Summer Activities 3-4 • EMC 1030

Color a 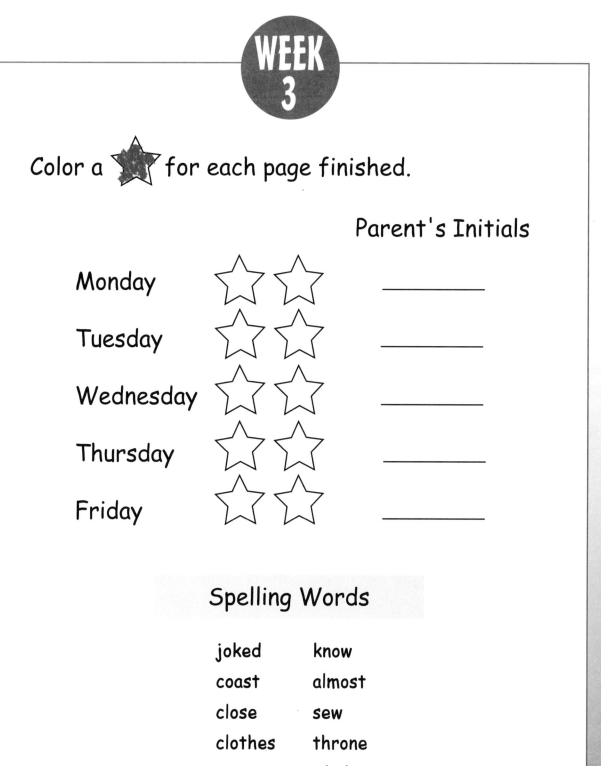 for each page finished.

Parent's Initials

Monday		_____
Tuesday		_____
Wednesday		_____
Thursday		_____
Friday		_____

Spelling Words

joked	know
coast	almost
close	sew
clothes	throne
wrote	whole

A Memorable Moment

What sticks in your mind about this week? Write about it.

_____

_____

_____

_____

_____

_____

Keeping Track

Color a book for every 15 minutes you read.

| Monday | Tuesday | Wednesday | Thursday | Friday |

Think about the books you read this week. Tell about a character's problem and how it was solved.

_____

_____

_____

_____

_____

The Golden Touch

King Midas was a greedy man. He loved gold more than anything in the world. One day, as King Midas finished counting his gold coins, he said grumpily, "I wish that everything I touch would turn to gold."

Suddenly, a strange feeling came over the king. He walked out into his garden and plucked a flower. The flower turned to solid gold. King Midas couldn't believe his eyes. He rushed around the palace, turning things to gold. "This is wonderful!" he thought. "At last, I can have all the gold I want!"

King Midas told his servants to bring him a fabulous feast to celebrate his amazing golden touch. King Midas sat down to eat. He picked up a piece of bread. It turned to gold. He chose a piece of fruit and it turned to gold. King Midas became frightened. "How will I eat?" he cried out.

His little daughter heard his cry and came running. Without thinking, the king opened his arms to his beloved daughter. She turned to gold, as cold and lifeless as stone.

"This golden touch is a curse!" yelled King Midas. "And so is my love of gold. I do not want it anymore!" He wept wildly, and his tears of regret fell upon the little golden girl. She began to breathe and move. The king was overcome with relief.

He touched the roasted chicken sitting before him. It remained a roasted chicken. He touched the cat that was sitting near his feet. The cat purred and rubbed against him. King Midas laughed with joy.

From that day on, King Midas cared only for the real treasures in life and had little interest in his gold.

1. What does the word *greedy* mean? _____

2. In the course of the story, King Midas experiences several different feelings. Name some of these feelings.

_____

3. At the end of the story, we learn that King Midas has learned to care for the "real treasures in life." What do you think these "treasures" might be?

_____

©2005 by Evan-Moor Corp. • Daily Summer Activities 3-4 • EMC 1030

Write It Right

1. are you going to eat that there doughnut

_____

2. mom would you buy some gum for julie and I

_____

3. maria said I would like to go to

_____

MATH TIME

Find the answers.

6 x 7 =   9 x 5 =   15 ÷ 3 =   32 ÷ 4 =

9 ÷ 3 =   42 ÷ 6 =   9 x 4 =   45 ÷ 5 =

8 x 4 =   28 ÷ 7 =   6 x 6 =   5 x 7 =

18 ÷ 2 =   6 x 9 =   21 ÷ 3 =   8 x 8 =

4 x 7 =   7 x 6 =   36 ÷ 6 =   27 ÷ 3 =

©2005 by Evan-Moor Corp. • Daily Summer Activities 3-4 • EMC 1030

Spell It!

All of this week's spelling words contain the long o sound. Fill in each blank below with a letter or combination of letters to make some additional long o words.

bone

b____st   m____n   m____st

th____se   l____ne   h____me

v____te   h____le   thr____t

Underline each word that contains the long o sound in the sentences below. Then copy the sentences using your best handwriting.

The clown joked about his funny clothes.

_____

_____

Do you know how to sew?

_____

_____

Adjectives are words that describe people, places, and things. An adjective can tell how something looks. It can tell what color, what kind, or how many.

Match each phrase with its picture. Then circle each adjective.

a big tiger

a fuzzy chick

a sad face

a white snowflake

a tired kitten

MATH⊙TIME

Find the answers.

48	59	105	121	95	82	67
+ 37	+ 83	+ 67	+ 90	− 17	− 59	+ 35

144	67	172	116	35	127	184
+ 39	+ 76	− 59	− 46	− 29	+ 38	− 26

Another Unnamed Story

Salt is a mineral that forms in the earth. The kind of salt that is dug out of salt mines is actually a rock called *halite*. So every time you use a salt shaker, you are sprinkling tiny rocks on your food! Salt can also be evaporated from seawater. This method leaves a very pure salt that many people prefer because of its good taste.

Salt not only makes food taste good, it is very important to our health. Body cells need salt to stay alive. In fact, salt makes up almost one percent of our blood and cells. Animals need salt, too. Farmers often put blocks of salt in the fields for animals to lick.

Salt has many other uses. Salt has long been used in preserving foods because it is antiseptic, or germ-killing. Salt is also used in making glass, soap, and other products.

In Poland, there are some very famous and unusual salt mines. Here, for hundreds of years, miners have dug salt from deep beneath the earth's surface. They have carved elegant rooms and beautiful statues from the solid salt. Tourists visit the salt mines to view the salt statues.

Long ago, salt was valued very highly because it was important and hard to get. In many parts of the world today, salt is still prized as a symbol of purity and friendship.

1. A good title for this story is

    a. Farm Animals   c. The Story of Salt

    b. Rocks and Minerals   d. Making Food Taste Good

2. The word *antiseptic* means _____

    _____

3. Name three important uses for salt.

    _____

    _____

    _____

Language Bytes

Antonyms are words that have opposite meanings. *Cold* and *hot*, *soft* and *hard*, and *up* and *down* are examples of antonyms. Write an antonym for each word below.

short _____   tame _____

good _____   sweet _____

old _____   sharp _____

dirty _____   slow _____

awake _____   happy _____

MATH TIME

Find the answers.

3 x 5 =   32 ÷ 4 =   40 ÷ 8 =   54 ÷ 6 =

24 ÷ 6 =   9 x 6 =   9 x 4 =   21 ÷ 7 =

16 ÷ 4 =   9 x 5 =   8 x 9 =   6 x 6 =

3 x 4 =   30 ÷ 6 =   7 x 6 =   4 x 8 =

7 x 3 =   7 x 9 =   81 ÷ 9 =   15 ÷ 5 =

©2005 by Evan-Moor Corp. • Daily Summer Activities 3-4 • EMC 1030

Geography

Here is a map of the 48 contiguous states of the United States.
Use an atlas or a globe to complete the jobs below.

Locate and label the U.S. capital.

Locate and label these states:
Florida, Illinois, Colorado,
Washington, and Connecticut.

In My Own Words

Combine each pair of sentences to make one sentence.

1. Joan went shopping for new shoes. Sue went shopping for new shoes.

_____

_____

2. Michelle packed for a trip to Mexico. At the same time, Chloe read a book.

_____

_____

Thursday

Week 3

41

MATH TIME

12	10	20	22	11	31	22
x 3	x 5	x 2	x 4	x 6	x 3	x 4

43	11	23	10	20	14	30
x 2	x 9	x 3	x 8	x 3	x 2	x 2

Rhyming words have the same ending sound. List at least three rhyming words for each word below.

bead _____ _____ _____

gate _____ _____ _____

hill _____ _____ _____

Make up a poem using some or all of your rhyming words.

_____

_____

_____

_____

Week 3

Thursday

©2005 by Evan-Moor Corp. • Daily Summer Activities 3-4 • EMC 1030

Language Bytes

Use a dictionary to find the definition of each word below. Then draw a picture to illustrate each definition.

hilarious

slumber

MATH TIME

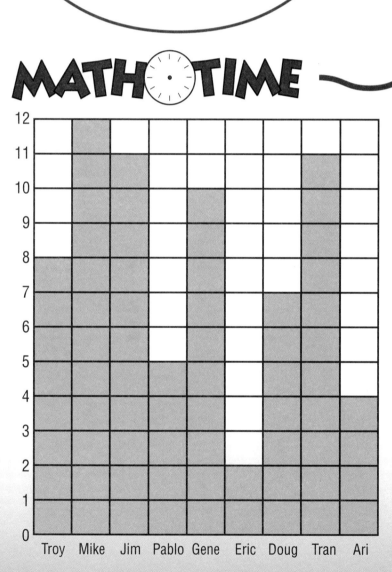

Use this information and the graph to answer the questions.

The basketball team at Great Falls High School kept track of the points scored by each player in Saturday's game. The information is shown in the graph. Use the information on the graph to answer the questions.

1. What was the total number of points scored?

_____

2. How many team members did not score any points?

_____

3. Which team member scored the most points?

_____

Friday

Week 3

43

zingoes

These are zingoes.

These are not zingoes.

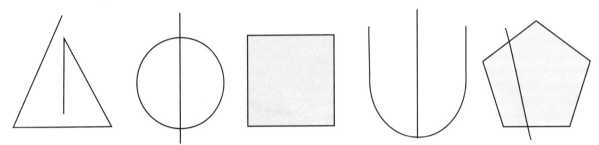

Circle the zingoes. Make an X on the items that are not zingoes.

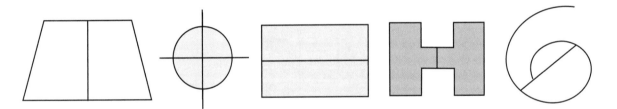

Draw three zingoes of your own in this box.

How do you know if something is a zingo?

_____

_____

©2005 by Evan-Moor Corp. • Daily Summer Activities 3-4 • EMC 1030

Color a ⭐ for each page finished.

Parent's Initials

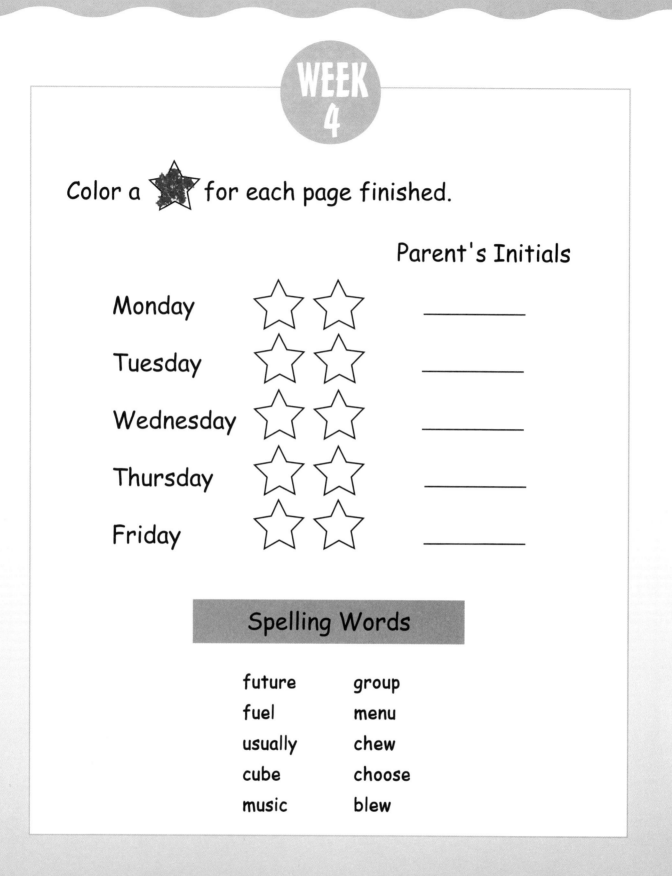

Monday

Tuesday

Wednesday

Thursday

Friday

_____

_____

_____

_____

_____

Spelling Words

future	group
fuel	menu
usually	chew
cube	choose
music	blew

A Memorable Moment

What sticks in your mind about this week? Write about it.

_____

_____

_____

_____

_____

_____

Keeping Track

Color a book for every 15 minutes you read.

Monday	Tuesday	Wednesday	Thursday	Friday

List four events from a book you are reading. Put them in the order in which they happened.

_____

_____

_____

_____

_____

A Day at the Zoo

Aunt Sally and Sheldon went to the zoo. They had fun looking at all the animals. They laughed at five little brown monkeys that did acrobatic tricks in the tree branches. They watched while three big white polar bears slid into a swimming pool. They counted as the zookeeper fed twelve shiny silver mackerel to the hungry seals. In the enormous reptile house, they gasped at the huge green anaconda snake that was over twenty feet long.

After looking at the snakes, Sheldon and Aunt Sally decided that they were ready to take a break. They each drank one large glass of pink lemonade and ate two small slices of pizza. When they finished eating, they threw their trash into a bright red trash can and headed off to see the elephants.

List five words from the story that name **sizes**.

_____

_____

_____

_____

_____

List five words from the story that name **colors**.

_____

_____

_____

_____

_____

List five words from the story that name **numbers**.

_____

_____

_____

_____

_____

List five words from the story that name animals.

_____

_____

_____

_____

_____

©2005 by Evan-Moor Corp. • Daily Summer Activities 3-4 • EMC 1030

Write It Right

1. our dad dont like to watch television

_____

2. the school bus arrives at sandpoint school at 810 in the morning

_____

_____

3. theirs a fire in the building

_____

MATH TIME

Find the answers.

48	65	57	83	104	56	66
− 19	+ 37	+ 94	− 65	− 28	+ 29	+ 46
77	91	44	132	125	92	147
+ 43	− 28	+ 39	− 46	+ 55	− 38	+ 49
123	104	45	38	75	136	108
− 64	+ 28	+ 38	+ 56	− 49	− 87	− 68

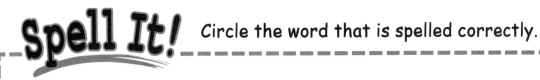

Spell It!

Circle the word that is spelled correctly.

1. The new car needs premium _____.

| fuel | fooel | fewel |

2. My dad says it is rude to _____ with your mouth open.

| choo | chue | chew |

3. After school, we like to listen to _____.

| muesic | music | mewsic |

4. The wind _____ our canoe into the middle of the lake.

| blew | blue | bluw |

5. No one can be sure what will happen in the _____.

| fewture | footure | future |

Copy this menu using your best handwriting.

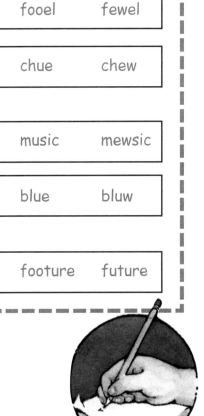

Ruby's Cafe Menu
Onion Soup
Stewed Mushrooms
New Potatoes
Cheese Cubes

Pronouns are words that take the place of nouns. Here are some pronouns that you already know:

she   he   it   we   they

Write the correct pronoun on each line.

1. Martin has a bicycle. _____ likes to ride _____.

2. Roger and Emily made some gingerbread.

    _____ put whipped cream on _____.

3. Elizabeth ran after the ball. _____ caught _____.

MATH⊙TIME   Find the answers.

16	31	52	45	63	52	63
x 4	x 6	x 3	x 2	x 5	x 4	x 6
29	72	65	94	80	21	15
x 3	x 2	x 3	x 2	x 4	x 6	x 2

©2005 by Evan-Moor Corp. • Daily Summer Activities 3-4 • EMC 1030

John Glenn

John Glenn was the first American to orbit the Earth in a spacecraft. On February 20, 1962, John traveled all the way around the Earth three times. The trip, in a spacecraft called *Friendship 7*, took about five hours.

When the trip was over, the spacecraft fired some rockets designed to push it out of orbit. The spacecraft hurtled toward the ocean. A large parachute opened, and the *Friendship 7* dropped gently into the Atlantic Ocean. A large United States Navy ship was waiting nearby. When John climbed out, safe and sound, the nation rejoiced. Many people said that John Glenn was a hero.

John Glenn would probably have said that he was just a regular guy. He was born in 1921. He grew up in Ohio, went to school, and then on to college. When World War II started, John signed up to be a Marine Corps pilot. He served in World War II and in the Korean War. He was awarded many medals for his service. After that, John became a test pilot and, eventually, an astronaut.

John Glenn went on to become a United States senator from Ohio. In 1998, as a crew member of the space shuttle *Discovery*, he became the oldest person to fly in space. He was 77 years old.

John Glenn has made space history twice in his life. Not bad for a "regular guy."

1. How did John Glenn make space history?

_____

_____

2. Do you think John Glenn is a hero? Explain your answer.

_____

_____

3. What does the word *rejoiced* mean?

_____

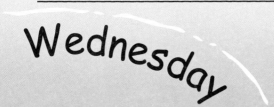

Wednesday   Week 4

Language Bytes

Replace the underlined word in each sentence with an antonym that makes more sense.

1. Jim lifts weights to make his muscles <u>weak</u>.

   _____

2. Callie put on a sweater because the weather was so <u>warm</u>.

   _____

3. The hungry dog wanted <u>less</u> food to eat.

   _____

4. Brad put a pad under his sleeping bag because the ground was so <u>soft</u>.

   _____

5. Our family eats lunch in the middle of the <u>night</u>.

   _____

MATH TIME   Find the answers.

1. Janice made bead necklaces to sell at the county fair. She worked for 30 days. She used 24 beads on each necklace. She made 6 necklaces each day.

   How many beads did she use each day?   _____

   How many necklaces did she make altogether?   _____

2. On the first day of the fair, Janice sold 52 necklaces for $3 each. How much money did she make that day?   _____

©2005 by Evan-Moor Corp. • Daily Summer Activities 3-4 • EMC 1030

Geography

Most maps include a symbol that looks something like this:

It is called a compass rose. It helps the reader find north, south, east, and west on the map.

Use the information on the compass rose to determine whether each statement below is true (T) or false (F).

_____ Lubbock is south of Amarillo.

_____ Wichita Falls is west of El Paso.

_____ Austin is west of San Antonio.

_____ Waco is north of Corpus Christi.

_____ Houston is north of Dallas.

_____ Beaumont is west of Fort Worth.

In My Own Words

A simile is a comparison between two objects or ideas. A simile always includes the word like or as. Here are some examples of similes:

> The baby's skin was as soft as velvet.

> The mulberry tree was like a giant, green umbrella.

Fill in the blanks to create your own similes.

The little boy was as _____ as a _____.

The cold wind felt like _____.

MATH ⏱ TIME

18	27	69	54	71	29	13
x 5	x 4	x 2	x 3	x 3	x 4	x 5

90	62	31	78	92	40	61
x 2	x 5	x 4	x 3	x 5	x 3	x 2

Language Bytes

Circle each pair of words that are synonyms. Draw a line under each pair of words that are antonyms.

tight	fast	smooth	pretty
loose	slow	rough	lovely

hard	easy	awake	moist
soft	simple	asleep	damp

Week 4

Thursday

©2005 by Evan-Moor Corp. • Daily Summer Activities 3-4 • EMC 1030

Language Bytes

Some pronouns are used to show ownership.

my   your   his   her   its   our   their

Fill in the blanks using the possessive pronouns above.

1. Please put _____ litter in the trash can.

2. Serena and Jesse found _____ lost dog.

3. Candace wants _____ birthday party to be special.

4. I have lots of fun with _____ best friend.

MATH TIME

Pick an apple from the tree to complete each number sentence.

$9 \times 2 =$ _____

_____ $\div 9 = 5$

$6 \times 6 =$ _____

$8 \times$ _____ $= 72$

$27 \div$ _____ $= 9$

$8 \times$ _____ $= 40$

_____ $\div 3 = 8$

$7 \times 8 =$ _____

Friday

Week 4

Elf Twins

Two of the elves on this page are twins.
They look exactly alike. Circle them.

©2005 by Evan-Moor Corp. • Daily Summer Activities 3-4 • EMC 1030

Color a ⭐ for each page finished.

Parent's Initials

Monday ☆☆ _____

Tuesday ☆☆ _____

Wednesday ☆☆ _____

Thursday ☆☆ _____

Friday ☆☆ _____

Spelling Words

we're	don't
I'll	wouldn't
aren't	won't
didn't	can't
doesn't	let's

A Memorable Moment

What sticks in your mind about this week?
Write about it.

_____

_____

_____

_____

Keeping Track

Color a book for every 15 minutes you read.

Monday	Tuesday	Wednesday	Thursday	Friday

Could the events in the book you are reading really happen?
Explain.

_____

_____

_____

_____

Growing Salad

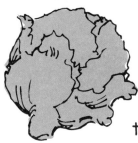

Steve, Brenda, Elena, and Renaldo worked together to plant a garden for their classroom. Steve and Brenda dug up the soil to loosen it. Renaldo raked the soil to remove the weeds and rocks. Elena bought seeds for the garden. She bought zucchini, carrot, lettuce, and radish seeds.

Each of the students chose one kind of seed to plant. Elena planted the zucchini seeds. Renaldo planted the carrot seeds. Brenda planted the lettuce seeds. Steve planted the radish seeds.

The four students took turns watering the garden. They all spent a few minutes each day pulling weeds. They were thrilled when the first tiny green sprouts appeared in the garden. The plants grew quickly. When the vegetables were ready, the gardening group proudly prepared and served a beautiful salad to their classmates.

Mark each statement with one of the following responses:

T = true   F = false   N = not enough information given in the story

_____ Five students worked together to make the garden.

_____ Renaldo enjoyed raking the soil.

_____ Brenda told Elena what kinds of seeds to buy.

_____ Steve planted the radish seeds.

_____ The lettuce seeds were the first to sprout.

_____ Brenda did not help pull weeds.

_____ Only Renaldo watered the garden.

_____ The salad tasted delicious.

_____ The salad looked beautiful.

_____ The gardening group felt good about their efforts.

Write It Right

1. last tuesday was warrens ninth birthday

_____

2. in april samantha took the train to augusta maine

_____

_____

3. he seen the movie titanic with us

_____

MATH TIME

Find the answers.

131 x 4	200 x 6	122 x 7	410 x 5	242 x 3	55 x 4
154 x 3	165 x 2	99 x 4	116 x 3	203 x 2	150 x 5

©2005 by Evan-Moor Corp. • Daily Summer Activities 3-4 • EMC 1030

 **Spell It!** Write the spelling words that are formed from these sets of words.

can not _____   we are _____

does not _____   did not _____

I will _____   would not _____

do not _____   will not _____

let us _____   are not _____

Copy the following sentences using your best handwriting.

A contraction combines two words into one. An apostrophe is placed in the contraction to show that a letter or letters are missing.

_____
- -
_____
- -
_____
- -
_____
- -
_____

Tuesday

Week 5

Language Bytes

Verbs are words that show action. Circle each word below that describes an action.

run	talk	book	lamp	eat	spin
dance	sit	jump	dog	catch	shirt
shoe	work	write	leap	orange	climb

 **MATH TIME** Fill in the missing numbers.

Complete each number sentence, both vertically and horizontally.

48	÷	8	=	
÷	✿	÷	✿	÷
6	÷	2	=	
=	✿	=	✿	=
	÷		=	

Week 5

Tuesday

©2005 by Evan-Moor Corp. • Daily Summer Activities 3-4 • EMC 1030

Nocturnal Animals

Did you know that when you go to bed at night, many animals are just beginning to stir? These animals sleep during much of the day and come out at night to hunt for food. Animals who are active during the hours of darkness are called *nocturnal* animals. Owls, raccoons, skunks, moths, mice, and bats are just a few of these animals.

You might think that it would be difficult for nocturnal animals to find their way around in the dark, but it isn't. Some of them have eyes that are specially formed to make use of moonlight and starlight. Their eyes are almost like mirrors that magnify the light and enable them to see quite well. Other animals rely on their noses. Mice, for example, use their sense of smell to guide them to food sources. Some animals rely on their ears. An owl can hear the soft rustling sound made by a mouse as it slips through the grass.

Go outside on a summer evening and sit quietly. Perhaps you will see or hear some nocturnal animals. Listen for the chirp of crickets. Watch the sky for a bat swooping after mosquitoes. Look around a porch light for moths and other insects that may be attracted to the glow. You might discover that nighttime brings a lot of action to your very own backyard!

1. What does *nocturnal* mean?

_____

_____

2. Mice use their sense of _____ to help them find food.

3. List three nocturnal animals you might see near your home.

_____   _____   _____

Wednesday

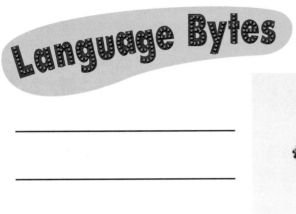

Make a list of at least four adjectives that describe the animal in the picture below.

_____   _____

_____   _____

_____   _____

Tell a story about the picture. Be sure to include your adjectives.

_____

_____

_____

_____

_____

Find the answers.

$3\overline{)21}$ $5\overline{)25}$ $9\overline{)36}$ $3\overline{)12}$ $4\overline{)16}$ $7\overline{)49}$

$8\overline{)64}$ $7\overline{)35}$ $5\overline{)40}$ $8\overline{)56}$ $3\overline{)27}$ $9\overline{)54}$

$6\overline{)30}$ $9\overline{)72}$ $7\overline{)63}$ $6\overline{)48}$ $5\overline{)45}$ $8\overline{)32}$

©2005 by Evan-Moor Corp. • Daily Summer Activities 3-4 • EMC 1030

Geography

The scale of the map lets the reader know how much real distance is represented on map.

Use the scale shown below to answer the questions. Use a ruler or estimate your answers.

About how far is it from Waterville to Brunswick?

_____

About how far is it from Lewiston to Augusta?

_____

About how far is it from Portand to Skowhegan?

_____

N
W   E
S

Skowhegan

Waterville

Augusta

Lewiston

Brunswick

Portland

Scale: $\frac{1}{4}$ inch = 25 miles

In My Own Words

Rewrite this run-on sentence as two or more sentences.

All the children in the class came to school on time and then they went on the field trip to the zoo and then they saw the lions, tigers, bears, and monkeys.

_____

_____

_____

_____

MATH TIME

57 _____   42 _____   16 _____

88 _____   95 _____   23 _____

169 _____   204 _____   131 _____

Language Bytes

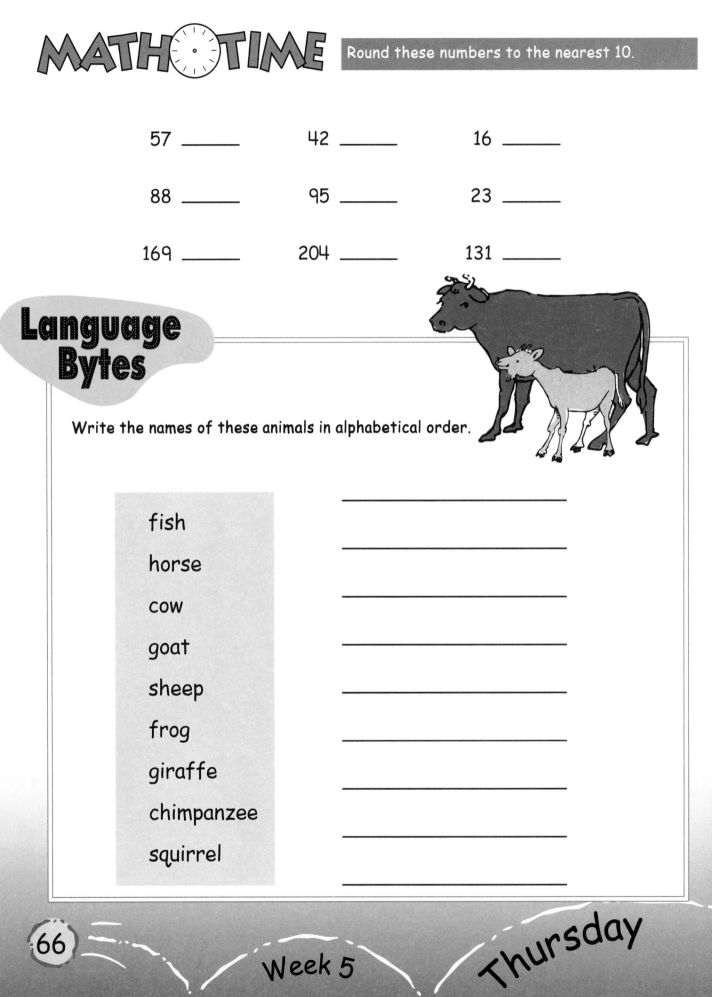

Write the names of these animals in alphabetical order.

| fish |
| horse |
| cow |
| goat |
| sheep |
| frog |
| giraffe |
| chimpanzee |
| squirrel |

_____

_____

_____

_____

_____

_____

_____

_____

_____

©2005 by Evan-Moor Corp. • Daily Summer Activities 3-4 • EMC 1030

Spell It!

Fill in each blank below using any verb that makes sense in the sentence. Try to make your verbs "colorful." For example, instead of *ate*, you might choose *gobbled*.

1. The baby likes to _____ across the carpet.

2. The mouse _____ away from the cat.

3. Joe and Carol went to the lake to _____ in the water.

4. Mac knows how to _____ the basketball.

5. The horse _____ across the meadow.

MATH TIME

Find the answers.

1. Selena's father made cookies for a class party.
   He made 3 cookies for each student in the class.
   He made 75 cookies altogether. How many students
   are in Selena's class?   _____

2. Cans of lemonade are on sale at Dailey's Market at
   2 cans for 88¢. What is the cost of one can of lemonade?   _____

3. Benny the baker is making a wedding cake. The cake is
   going to have 5 layers. He needs 12 eggs for each layer.
   How many eggs does he need?   _____

Forest Maze

Help the lost hiker find his way through the forest and back to his tent.

Week 5

Friday

Color a ⭐ for each page finished.

Parent's Initials

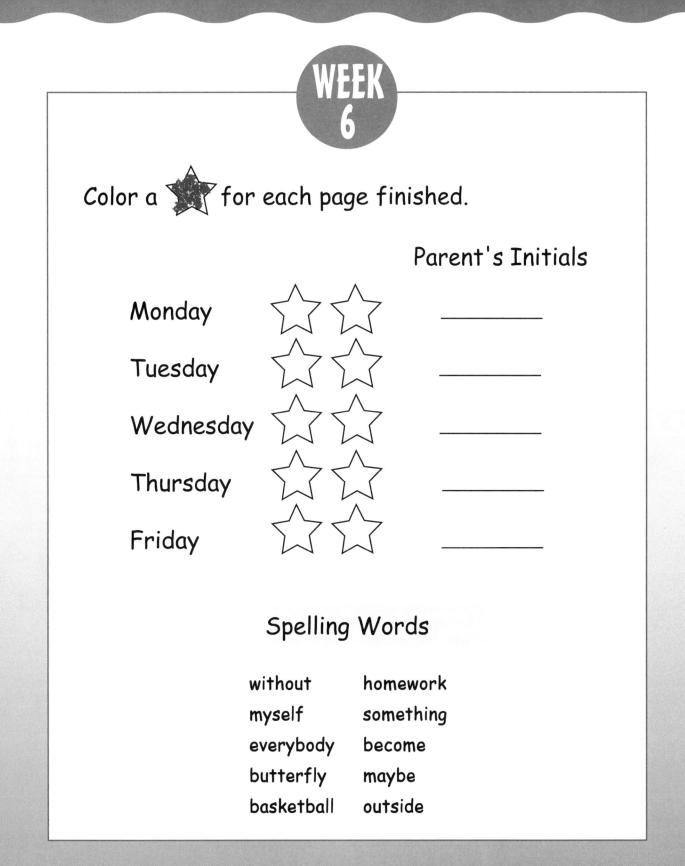

Monday ☆ ☆ _____

Tuesday ☆ ☆ _____

Wednesday ☆ ☆ _____

Thursday ☆ ☆ _____

Friday ☆ ☆ _____

Spelling Words

without	homework
myself	something
everybody	become
butterfly	maybe
basketball	outside

A Memorable Moment

What sticks in your mind about this week?
Write about it.

_____

_____

_____

_____

_____

_____

Keeping Track

Color a book for every 15 minutes you read.

Monday	Tuesday	Wednesday	Thursday	Friday

Describe a character you read about this week.

_____

_____

_____

_____

_____

_____

Can you create a story?

Number the parts of this story in order from 1 to 9 to make a sensible story.

_____ Jamie's mother was waiting outside the school. Jamie and her two best friends, Sarah and Tonya, climbed happily into the car.

_____ Everyone sat down to a big spaghetti dinner, topped off with cake and ice cream.

_____ On Friday afternoon, Jamie could hardly keep her mind on the spelling lesson.

_____ After dinner the girls watched a funny movie in the den.

_____ Jamie's mother drove the girls to the skating rink. They skated for two hours. Then Jamie's father came to drive them back to Jamie's house.

_____ She was too excited about her birthday party. Finally, the bell rang and school was over.

_____ In the morning, Jamie's father made pancakes for breakfast, and then Jamie's mother drove Sarah and Tonya home.

_____ As they walked in the door, they smelled something wonderful. It was spaghetti, Jamie's favorite food.

_____ When the movie was over, the girls spread out their sleeping bags on the floor and went to sleep.

Write It Right

1. dont you want to climb mount johnson

_____

_____

2. dr palmer has went to the hospital all ready

_____

_____

3. ella sang a song called its a beautiful day

_____

_____

MATH TIME

Find the answers.

$2\overline{)19}$ $\qquad$ $3\overline{)17}$ $\qquad$ $4\overline{)26}$ $\qquad$ $5\overline{)28}$ $\qquad$ $8\overline{)76}$ $\qquad$ $4\overline{)34}$

$6\overline{)44}$ $\qquad$ $9\overline{)64}$ $\qquad$ $6\overline{)47}$ $\qquad$ $5\overline{)39}$ $\qquad$ $2\overline{)13}$ $\qquad$ $5\overline{)46}$

Week 6

Monday

©2005 by Evan-Moor Corp. • Daily Summer Activities 3-4 • EMC 1030

Spell It!

Your spelling words this week are all compound words. Match each word on the left with a word on the right to make a spelling word.

with	body
my	be
every	come
butter	work
basket	out
home	thing
some	side
be	ball
may	fly
out	self

Circle the compound words used in this poem. Then copy the poem using your best handwriting.

The sunflowers waved in the summer breeze.
A rainbow painted the sky.
A grasshopper jumped from leaf to leaf,
And a butterfly floated by.

Language Bytes

Homophones are words that sound alike but are spelled differently and have different meanings.

Complete each pair of sentences using a pair of homophones.

1. The robber tried to _____ the jewelry.

   The bridge was built of _____.

2. I read a fairy _____ to my niece.

   The cat's _____ twitches when she sees a mouse.

3. The belt fits around his _____.

   My family is careful not to _____ food.

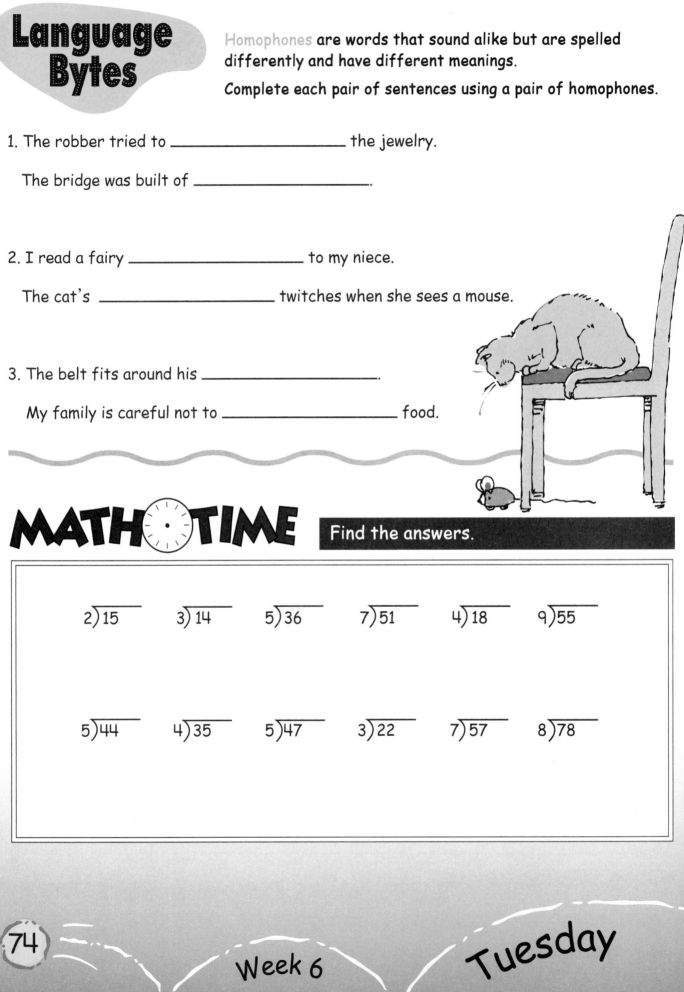

MATH TIME

Find the answers.

$2\overline{)15}$ $3\overline{)14}$ $5\overline{)36}$ $7\overline{)51}$ $4\overline{)18}$ $9\overline{)55}$

$5\overline{)44}$ $4\overline{)35}$ $5\overline{)47}$ $3\overline{)22}$ $7\overline{)57}$ $8\overline{)78}$

©2005 by Evan-Moor Corp. • Daily Summer Activities 3-4 • EMC 1030

Jane Goodall

When Jane Goodall was twenty-six years old, she began a great adventure. The year was 1960. Jane went to Africa on a special project. Her job was to learn everything she could about chimpanzees. She set up her camp on a game reserve. (A game reserve is an area that has been set aside as a place where animals can live freely and safely.)

Jane went out into the forest every day. She sat and watched the chimpanzees for hours at a time. She wrote down every detail of their behavior. She got to know the chimpanzees very well. After a time, they came to trust her and accept her as a friend.

Jane's work led to several new discoveries. She found that chimpanzees use tools to get food. She watched as they poked sticks into termite holes to gather insects to eat. She also learned that chimpanzees sometimes hunt small animals for meat. This was a big surprise. Scientists had always thought that chimpanzees ate only fruit and vegetation.

National Geographic has produced many films and articles about Jane Goodall's work. Jane has also written books about her experiences.

Jane Goodall has dedicated her life to helping expand humankind's knowledge and understanding of animals. She continues her work today through the Jane Goodall Institute. To learn more, contact the Jane Goodall Institute at 8700 Georgia Ave., Suite 500, Silver Spring, Maryland 20910.

1. Why did Jane Goodall go to Africa?

   _____

   _____

2. What surprising discoveries did Jane make?

   _____

   _____

3. This article is mostly about Jane Goodall's
   a. books   b. friends   c. work

Week 6

©2005 by Evan-Moor Corp. • Daily Summer Activities 3-4 • EMC 1030

Language Bytes

Verbs can have different forms. A verb in the **present tense** tells an action that **happens now.** A verb in the past tense tells about an action that already happened.

Match each present tense verb with its past tense verb.

run	sang
swim	laughed
play	slid
speak	hopped
laugh	ran
hop	spoke
sing	swam
slide	played

MATH TIME

Find the answers.

Fill in each blank using a unit of measurement that makes sense in the sentence.

1. I worked on my book report for 2 _____ last night.

2. My father is 6 _____ tall.

3. The distance to my grandmother's house is 50 _____.

4. Jorge went to the store to buy a _____ of milk and 5 _____ of sugar.

5. Mr. Fitch is 63 _____ old.

6. The package was 12 _____ wide.

7. The recipe calls for 3 _____ of flour.

©2005 by Evan-Moor Corp. • Daily Summer Activities 3-4 • EMC 1030

Geography

Maps can give us all kinds of information. This map of China uses color to show the average amounts of rainfall in different parts of that country.

Use the information contained in the key. Circle the correct answers.

The northeast southeast area of China receives the most rainfall.

Dark blue indicates the greatest least amount of rainfall.

An average rainfall of 20 to 40 inches is represented by which color?

a. [____] b. [____] c. [____]

Rainfall in China

Rainfall in Inches

more than 80
60–80
40–60
20–40
4–20
less than 4

In My Own Words

Write a paragraph explaining how to build a sand castle.
Include some of these words: *first, next, then, after that, finally.*

_____

_____

_____

_____

_____

_____

Thursday

Week 6

MATH TIME

1. 61   4   72   54   113   68

___   ___   ___   ___   ___   ___

2. 210   221   219   235   232   227

___   ___   ___   ___   ___   ___

3. 1,873   1,765   1,921   1,780   1,836   1,909

___   ___   ___   ___   ___   ___

Language Bytes

Adjectives make writing more interesting.

Choose interesting adjectives to complete each sentence below.
Make sure that the words you use make sense in the sentence.

1. The house had windows.

   The _____ house had _____ windows.

2. The cats licked their fur.

   The _____ cats licked their _____ fur.

3. Aunt Sophia stirred the stew with a spoon.

   Aunt Sophia stirred the _____ stew with a _____ spoon.

©2005 by Evan-Moor Corp. • Daily Summer Activities 3–4 • EMC 1030

Language Bytes

Number the words in each list in alphabetical order from 1 to 5.

_____ termite	_____ macaroni	_____ different
_____ team	_____ magazine	_____ dice
_____ tennis	_____ marigold	_____ divide
_____ ten	_____ maple	_____ dishes
_____ temper	_____ maid	_____ dim

MATH TIME

Find the answers.

$3\overline{)28}$ $4\overline{)24}$ $5\overline{)42}$ $6\overline{)38}$ $6\overline{)57}$ $9\overline{)75}$

$6\overline{)46}$ $7\overline{)57}$ $8\overline{)69}$ $9\overline{)82}$ $5\overline{)49}$ $3\overline{)29}$

$7\overline{)53}$ $4\overline{)25}$ $8\overline{)67}$ $7\overline{)19}$ $9\overline{)81}$ $7\overline{)29}$

©2005 by Evan-Moor Corp. • Daily Summer Activities 3-4 • EMC 1030

What's wrong with this picture?

There are many things wrong with this park scene.
Find them. Tell someone what you found.

Color a  for each page finished.

Parent's Initials

Monday ☆ ☆ _____

Tuesday ☆ ☆ _____

Wednesday ☆ ☆ _____

Thursday ☆ ☆ _____

Friday ☆ ☆ _____

Spelling Words

ground	tough
around	bought
would	joined
should	pointing
rough	choice

A Memorable Moment

What sticks in your mind about this week? Write about it.

_____

_____

_____

_____

_____

_____

Keeping Track

Color a book for every 15 minutes you read.

Monday	Tuesday	Wednesday	Thursday	Friday

Describe the setting of a story you read this week.

_____

_____

_____

_____

_____

_____

Title: _____

Annie looked out the window. It was starting to snow. Big, fluffy, white flakes were drifting down. Soon the ground was frosted with white. Annie stood at the window and watched until it began to grow dark outside. She was thinking about snowmen. Annie loved making snowmen with her dad, and tomorrow they could make their first snowman of the season.

When Annie woke up the next morning, sunshine was streaming through her bedroom window. Her dad was already up and dressed. He came into her room with the smell of cold, fresh air clinging to his coat. He had a mug of hot chocolate in his hand. "Wake up, sleepyhead," he said, smiling. "The snow is two feet deep!"

Annie sprang out of her bed and pulled on warm pants and a sweater. She sipped the hot chocolate while her dad spooned oatmeal into bowls for each of them. While they ate, they talked about the snowman they would build. This year, they decided, they would make the biggest snowman ever!

1. During what season of the year does this story take place? _____

2. What time of day was it when the snow began to fall?

    a. early morning

    b. late afternoon

    c. midnight

3. Write a good title for this story in the box above the story.

4. What do you think might happen next in the story?

_____

_____

_____

Monday

Week 7

1. father and me eat the pancakes yesterday

_____

2. uncle sylvester wear a funny costume last halloween

_____

_____

3. our class we had fun going threw the museum

_____

_____

MATH TIME

Find the answers.

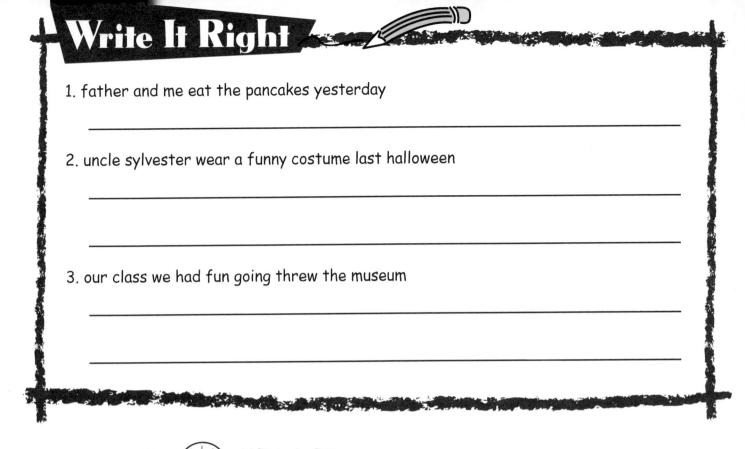

40	33	52	100	67	35	13
x 2	x 1	x 8	x 4	x 2	x 9	x 3

94	28	71	86	18	82	60
x 2	x 4	x 9	x 6	x 8	x 5	x 7

©2005 by Evan-Moor Corp. • Daily Summer Activities 3-4 • EMC 1030

Spell It!

Fill in each blank with ou or oi to make one of this week's spelling words. Then say the words aloud.

gr_____nd   r_____gh

t_____gh   b_____ght

w_____ld   p_____nting

sh_____ld   ar_____nd

ch_____ce   j_____ned

oi

ou

How many different sounds can you hear for the ou combination? _____

What other letter combination makes the oi sound? _____

Use your best handwriting to copy these place names.

United States of America

_____

- - - - - - - - - - - - - - - - - -

Yellowstone National Park

_____

- - - - - - - - - - - - - - - - - -

Lake Michigan

_____

- - - - - - - - - - - - - - - - - -

New Orleans, Louisiana

_____

- - - - - - - - - - - - - - - - - -

Language Bytes

Adverbs are words that tell how, when, or where things happen. Some adverbs are listed below. Decide whether each word tells how, when, or where and write it under the correct heading.

How	When	Where
_____	_____	_____
_____	_____	_____
_____	_____	_____
_____	_____	_____

anywhere	sweetly	never	there
sometimes	here	today	everywhere
softly	early	sadly	bravely

MATH TIME

Find the answers.

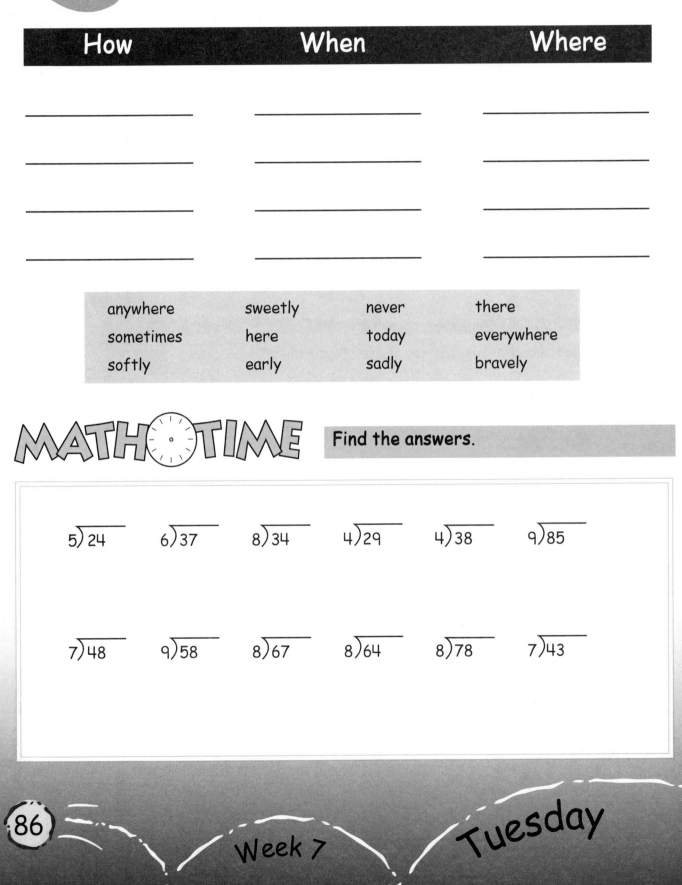

$5\overline{)24}$ $6\overline{)37}$ $8\overline{)34}$ $4\overline{)29}$ $4\overline{)38}$ $9\overline{)85}$

$7\overline{)48}$ $9\overline{)58}$ $8\overline{)67}$ $8\overline{)64}$ $8\overline{)78}$ $7\overline{)43}$

The Planet Mars

Mars is the fourth planet in our solar system. It is about 142 million miles away from the sun. You can often see Mars in the sky. It looks like a bright, reddish star. The red color comes from the red dust on the surface of the planet. This dust is often swirled into the thin atmosphere on Mars by fierce windstorms.

Mars is a fairly small planet. It is about one-half the size of Earth. The north and south poles of the planet are covered with ice and snow. Mars has volcanoes, mountains, canyons, and craters. There are odd lines and streaks on the surface of Mars that some scientists think may be old riverbeds. Mars has two small moons.

Space vehicles have been sent to Mars to take pictures and collect soil samples. Recently, scientists found evidence that there may have been simple life-forms on Mars at some time in the past. They examined rocks from Mars that seemed to contain the remains of some bacteria. Scientists continue to study and learn more about Mars. Someday, people from Earth may even visit our neighboring planet.

Mark each statement true (T) or false (F).

_____ Mars is larger than Earth.

_____ Mars can be seen from Earth.

_____ Mars is the fourth planet in the solar system.

_____ The surface of Mars is covered with red dust.

_____ Scientists think large animals once lived on Mars.

_____ The surface of Mars is very smooth and flat.

_____ Mars is a star.

©2005 by Evan-Moor Corp. • Daily Summer Activities 3-4 • EMC 1030

Language Bytes

An analogy compares two sets of items. An analogy contains the words **is to** and **as**. For example:

big is to **small** as **hot** is to **cold**

To make it quicker to write an analogy, symbols can be used. In place of **is to**, we can use **:**. In place of **as**, we can use **::**.

Complete these analogies.

kitten : cat : : calf : _____

snow : cold : : fire : _____

sugar : sweet : : lemon : _____

light : day : : dark : _____

hop : rabbit : : gallop : _____

spoon : stir : : shovel : _____

MATH TIME

Find the answers.

Mr. Manilla helped his class create a graph showing their favorite kinds of cookies. Use the information on the graph to answer the questions below.

☐ = 1 student

chocolate chip										
waffle crème										
peanut butter										
oatmeal										
gingersnap										

Which cookie is the most popular? _____

Which cookie is the least popular? _____

How many students like chocolate chip cookies best? _____

How many students participated in creating the graph? _____

(88)

Week 7   Wednesday

Ge☀graphy

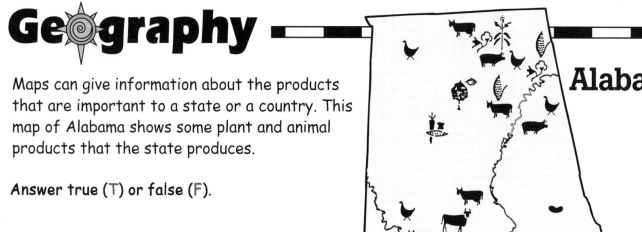

Alabama

Maps can give information about the products that are important to a state or a country. This map of Alabama shows some plant and animal products that the state produces.

Answer true (T) or false (F).

_____ Peanuts are grown all over the state.

_____ Cotton is grown in more areas than corn.

_____ Animals are raised in most parts of the state.

_____ Corn is grown in the areas where hogs are raised.

_____ Twice as many dairy cows as beef cattle are raised.

Legend

🐗	hogs	🌿	cotton
🐄	beef cattle	🌽	soybeans
🥜	peanuts	🐓	poultry
🌱	corn	🐄	dairy products

In My Own Words

Write a paragraph that describes the animal in the picture.

_____

_____

_____

_____

_____

_____

1. The Thingamabob Company received an order for
   56 Thingamabobs. Thingamabobs are packaged
   8 to a box. How many boxes of Thingamabobs will
   it take to fill the order?

   _____

2. Penelope works at the Thingamabob Company.
   She worked 36 hours last week. She made
   9 Thingamabobs. How long did it take Penelope
   to make 1 Thingamabob?

   _____

Language Bytes

Circle the one word in each group that tells about
all the other words in that group.

mice	Ralph	cake
frogs	Betty	food
animals	Fred	pizza
rabbits	people	apple
birds	Shirley	bread

Write a sentence using all three of the circled words.

_____

_____

©2005 by Evan-Moor Corp. • Daily Summer Activities 3-4 • EMC 1030

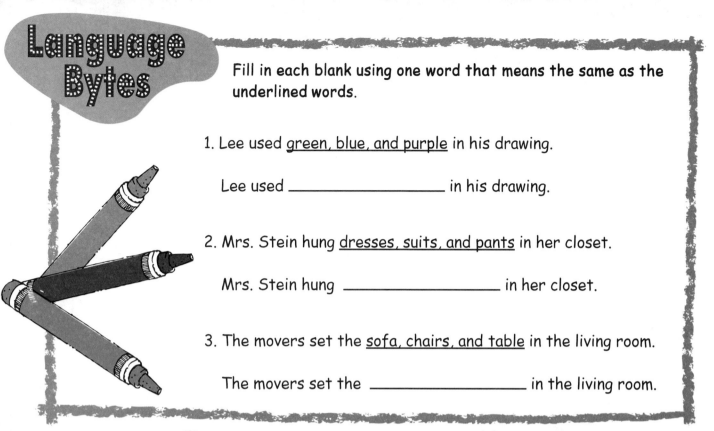

Language Bytes

Fill in each blank using one word that means the same as the underlined words.

1. Lee used green, blue, and purple in his drawing.

   Lee used _____ in his drawing.

2. Mrs. Stein hung dresses, suits, and pants in her closet.

   Mrs. Stein hung _____ in her closet.

3. The movers set the sofa, chairs, and table in the living room.

   The movers set the _____ in the living room.

MATH TIME

Use the calendar and the clues to answer the questions.

1. The first day of school is on a Tuesday. It is after September 1 but before September 10. The first day of school is

   _____.

SEPTEMBER						
SUN	**MON**	**TUE**	**WED**	**THU**	**FRI**	**SAT**
			1	2	3	4
5	6	7	8	9	10	11
12	13	14	15	16	17	18
19	20	21	22	23	24	25
26	27	28	29	30		

2. Louella's birthday is on a Wednesday. It is not the first or last Wednesday of the month. It is more than two weeks after school starts. Louella's birthday is

   _____.

3. The first football game of the season is on a Saturday. It is after school starts but before Louella's birthday. It is in the first half of the month. The first football game is

   _____.

Week 7

Picture Crossword

Solve this crossword puzzle by writing the name of each object in the correct place on the puzzle grid.

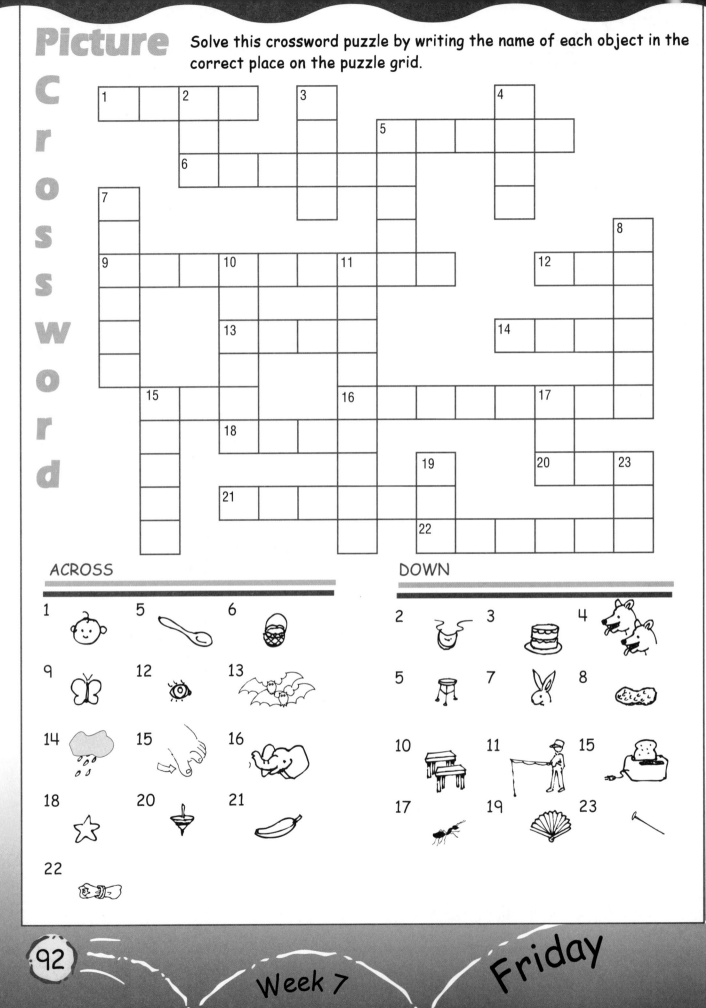

ACROSS

DOWN

Week 7

Friday

Color a  for each page finished.

Parent's Initials

Monday ☆ ☆ _____

Tuesday ☆ ☆ _____

Wednesday ☆ ☆ _____

Thursday ☆ ☆ _____

Friday ☆ ☆ _____

Spelling Words

ghost	climb
gnaw	limb
right	neighbor
knew	knight
wrong	hour

A Memorable Moment

What sticks in your mind about this week? Write about it.

_____

_____

_____

_____

_____

_____

Keeping Track

Color a book for every 15 minutes you read.

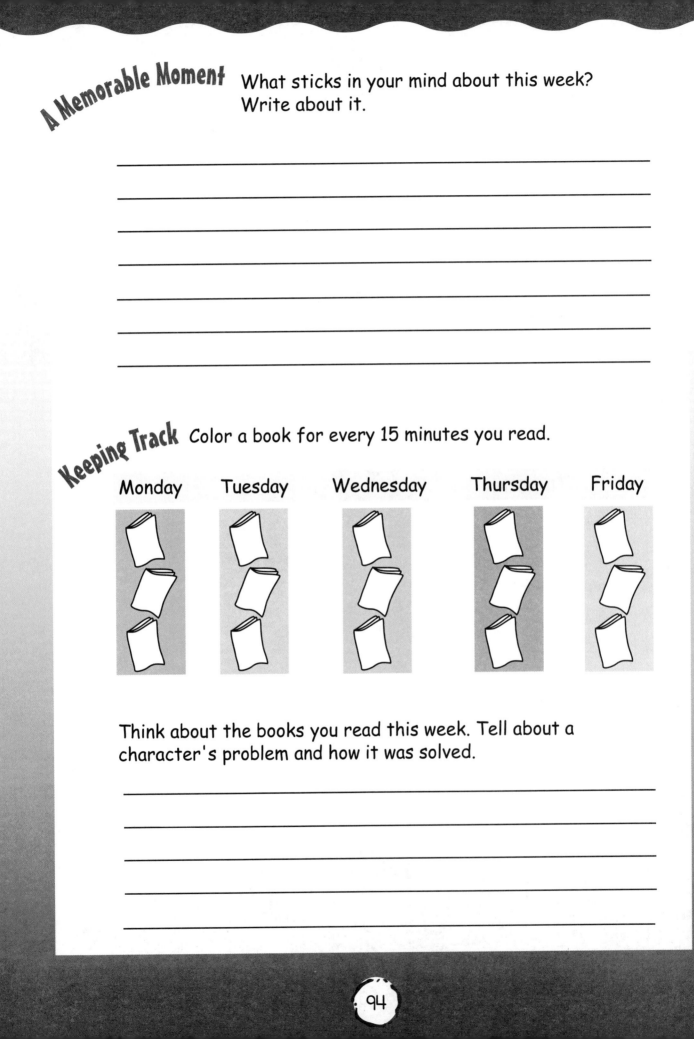

Monday	Tuesday	Wednesday	Thursday	Friday

Think about the books you read this week. Tell about a character's problem and how it was solved.

_____

_____

_____

_____

_____

The Boy Who Cried Wolf

Long ago, there was a young shepherd boy who tended the sheep on the hillside. He made sure that they stayed together and came to no harm.

The boy longed for a little excitement. To play a trick on the village people, he stood on a stump and yelled with all his might, "Wolf! Wolf! A wolf is after the sheep!"

The villagers stopped their work, grabbed rakes and good, stout sticks, and ran to the hillside. There they found the boy, laughing out loud at his funny joke. There was no wolf in sight.

The village people did not think it was funny. They scolded the boy for being foolish.

A few days later, the boy was more bored than ever. He wondered if his trick would work once more. So he stood on the same stump and yelled, "Wolf! Wolf! A wolf is after the sheep!"

Again the villagers came running, only to find that the boy was playing a joke. This time, they were very angry and told him to never, never play such a trick again.

The next day began peacefully. Then, all at once, a lean and hungry wolf appeared at the edge of the meadow. The wolf leaped among the sheep, killing a lamb in an instant. The boy jumped to his stump and yelled, "Wolf! Wolf! A wolf is after the sheep!"

The villagers heard his cry and said, "He can't fool us again." They simply smiled and went on with their work. The poor boy could only stand and watch while the wolf devoured his sheep.

1. The word *devoured* means _____.

2. This story teaches that it is important to

   a. work hard   b. get up early   c. tell the truth

3. Why didn't the villagers help the boy when the wolf came?

_____

Write It Right

1. sami ate three hot dogs and drank too sodas

_____

_____

2. have you ever done been to the nebraska state fair

`_____

_____

3. ming shouted wait for me

_____

MATH TIME

Find the answers.

124	39	87	95	64	82
x 4	x 3	x 2	x 5	x 3	x 5

$4\overline{)17}$ $7\overline{)65}$ $6\overline{)44}$ $7\overline{)24}$ $5\overline{)17}$ $6\overline{)33}$

©2005 by Evan-Moor Corp. • Daily Summer Activities 3-4 • EMC 1030

Spell It!

ghost   climb

gnaw   limb

right   neighbor

knew   knight

wrong   hour

Copy this poem using your best handwriting. Find at least three words in the poem that contain silent letters and circle them.

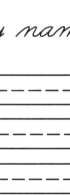

I'd like to live on an island
With the sparkling sea at my door.
I would gather shells in a basket
And write my name on the shore.

Language Bytes

Fill in each blank with a word that completes the rhyme and makes sense.

1. I climbed up a willow tree.

   I fell down and skinned my _____.

2. Susie made a birthday cake.

   She put it in the oven to _____.

3. Marta went for a ride on her bike.

   Julio and Tran took a nice, long _____.

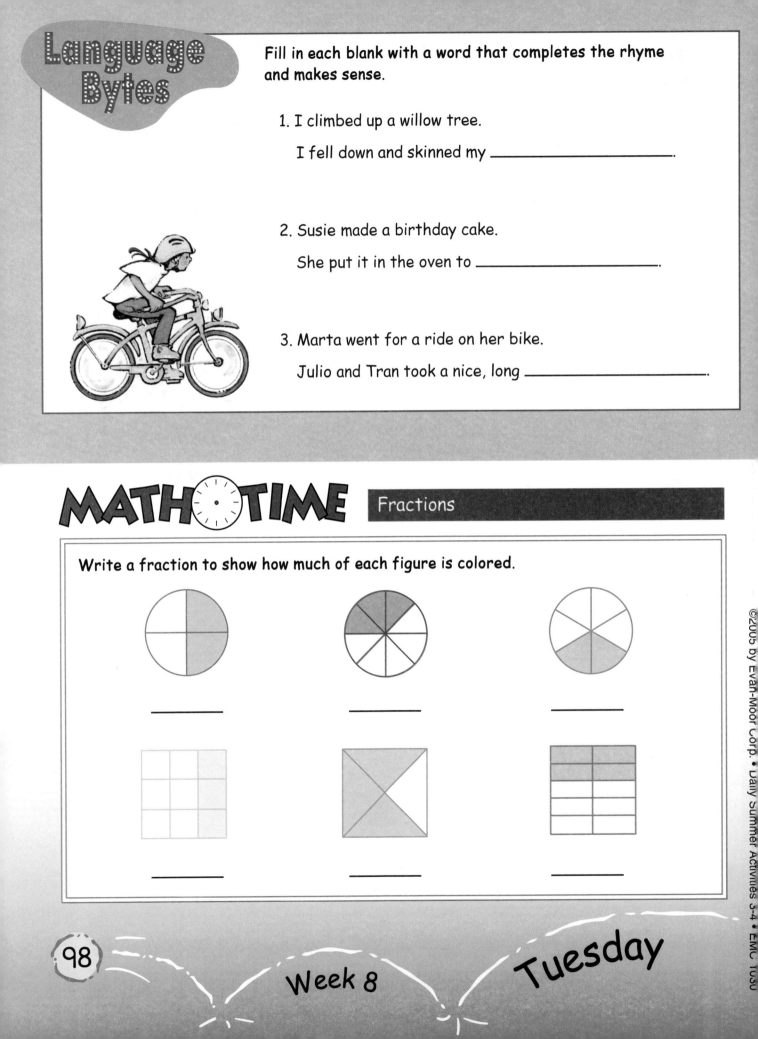

MATH TIME   Fractions

Write a fraction to show how much of each figure is colored.

_____   _____   _____

_____   _____   _____

A Great Civilization

The Aztecs were Native Americans who created a great civilization in the land that is now Mexico. During the 1400s and early 1500s, the Aztecs ruled a powerful empire. They built enormous cities. They made temples, sculptures, and carvings.

Religion was important to the Aztecs. They worshipped many gods and goddesses and held many different kinds of religious ceremonies.

The Aztecs were good farmers. Their main food was corn, which they made into tortillas, or thin, flat pieces of bread. They liked spicy chili peppers in their food. They hunted deer, rabbits, and birds for meat.

Aztec families lived in simple homes made of wood and adobe clay. Everyone in the family, including the children, had to help with chores. These included farming, cooking, weaving cloth, and sewing. Boys went to school for religious and military training. Girls were taught mostly at home.

The Aztec Empire came to an end when Spain invaded it in 1519. The Spanish soldiers destroyed most of the Aztecs' cities and buildings. Fortunately, a few buildings were saved, and many pieces of Aztec artwork are now on display in museums in Mexico City. People today are still fascinated by the Aztecs and their ancient way of life.

1. Who were the Aztecs and where did they live?

_____

2. What are some of the things the Aztecs did?

_____

3. About how many years ago did the Aztec Empire exist?

    a. 1,000   b. 250   c. 500

4. Why did the Aztec Empire come to an end?

_____

Language Bytes

Add an adverb to each sentence below. Make sure that the word you use makes sense. There are many possible answers.

Circle one.

This adverb tells:

1. Jane brushed her hair _____.

how   when   where

2. Mr. Picky chewed his food _____.

how   when   where

3. We looked around _____.

how   when   where

MATH TIME

Find the answers.

93	67	44	133	75	28
× 4	× 9	× 2	× 2	× 4	× 6

$6)\overline{30}$ $9)\overline{95}$ $4)\overline{11}$ $6)\overline{46}$ $7)\overline{19}$ $5)\overline{23}$

100

Week 8

Wednesday

©2005 by Evan-Moor Corp. • Daily Summer Activities 3-4 • EMC 1030

Geography

Pierre has found a treasure map. Follow the directions below to help him find the treasure. Make an X on that spot.

Begin at Mystic Mountain.

Go 3 spaces east.

Go 6 spaces north.

Follow the Riddle River 5 spaces east.

Go south 3 spaces and start digging.

Lake Gloomy

Riddle River

N
W　E
S

Endless Cavern

Fantasy Forest

Mystic Mountain

In My Own Words

Fill in the blanks in the sentence below. Then write a paragraph using the sentence as a topic sentence.

_____ is better than_____.

_____

_____

_____

Count each set of coins and write the amount. Match the coins to the correct person.

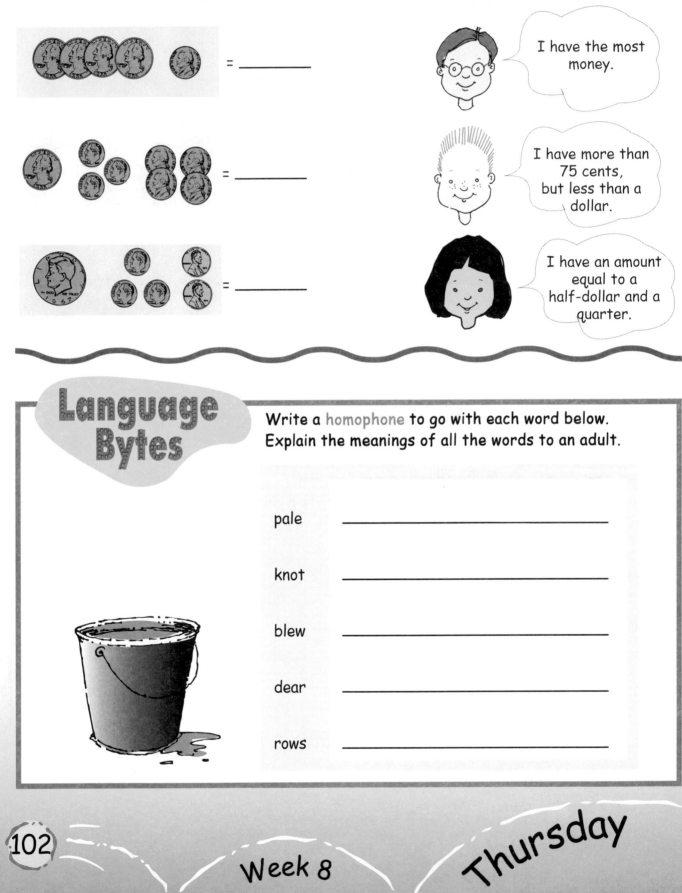

= _____

I have the most money.

= _____

I have more than 75 cents, but less than a dollar.

= _____

I have an amount equal to a half-dollar and a quarter.

Language Bytes

Write a homophone to go with each word below.
Explain the meanings of all the words to an adult.

pale _____

knot _____

blew _____

dear _____

rows _____

©2005 by Evan-Moor Corp. • Daily Summer Activities 3-4 • EMC 1030

Language Bytes

Choose the pronoun that best completes each sentence.

| She   I   He |

1. _____ want to go to the circus tomorrow.

| her   she   their |

2. John and Becky almost missed _____ flight.

| he   me   they |

3. Mario visited _____ at my ranch.

| me   he   they |

4. "I am a good baseball player," _____ said.

MATH TIME

Find the answers.

1. Sandy bought a melon that weighed 3 pounds. It cost 33¢ per pound. How much did she pay for the melon?

   _____

   Sandy paid for the melon with a $5 bill. How much change did she receive?

   _____

2. Jim bought some flowers. He bought 2 roses and 4 tulips. The roses cost $2 each. The tulips cost $1.50 each. How much did the flowers cost altogether?

   _____

Rebus Puzzle

In the workspace, spell out the names of the pictures in the top row. Then take away the letters of the pictures in the second row in order. Write the letters that are left in the answer box. You will spell the name of something that would give you a fast ride.

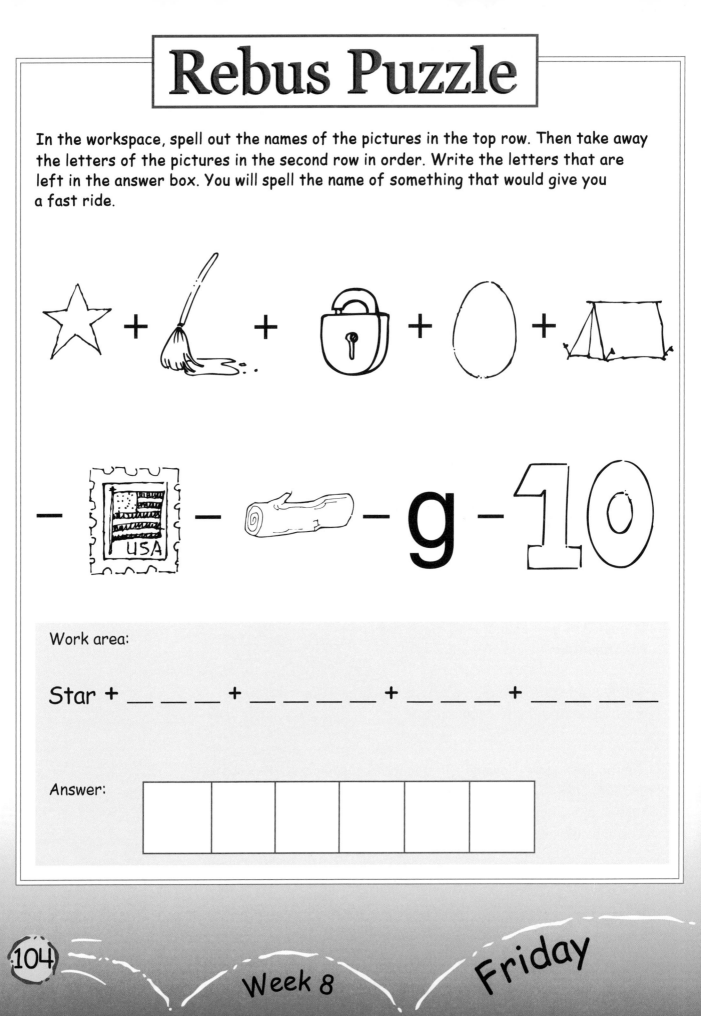

Work area:

Star + __ __ __ + __ __ __ __ + __ __ __ + __ __ __ __

Answer:

Color a ⭐ for each page finished.

Parent's Initials

		Parent's Initials
Monday	☆ ☆	_____
Tuesday	☆ ☆	_____
Wednesday	☆ ☆	_____
Thursday	☆ ☆	_____
Friday	☆ ☆	_____

Spelling Words

smarter	spelling
longer	playing
having	studied
smiling	turned
swimming	stirred

A Memorable Moment

What sticks in your mind about this week? Write about it.

_____

_____

_____

_____

_____

_____

Keeping Track

Color a book for every 15 minutes you read.

Monday	Tuesday	Wednesday	Thursday	Friday

List four events from a book you are reading. Put them in the order in which they happened.

_____

_____

_____

_____

_____

A Busy Trip

The Ryan family took a trip to New York City. First, they walked to the Empire State Building. Next, they took the ferry to the Statue of Liberty. After that, they rode the subway to Central Park. They ate lunch in the park and fed the pigeons. They bought ice-cream cones and then walked by the lake. Late in the afternoon, they took a taxi back to their hotel. After they had dinner, they went to a musical play.

Circle each correct answer.

Did the Ryans eat lunch before or after they saw the Statue of Liberty?

before   after

Did they take a taxi before or after they rode on the ferry?

before   after

Did they feed the pigeons before or after they rode the subway?

before   after

Did they have dinner before or after they went to a musical play?

before   after

Did they see the Empire State Building before or after they went to Central Park?

before   after

Did they buy ice-cream cones before or after they walked by the lake?

before   after

List all the ways the Ryans traveled while in New York City.

_____

_____

_____

Write It Right

1. my brother and me visited our aunt uncle and cousins in chicago

_____

_____

2. do you got a lot of home work tonight

_____

3. we new how to spell all the words on fridays test

_____

_____

MATH TIME

Find the answers.

61	73	92	10	54	88
+ 28	- 46	+ 37	+ 84	- 16	- 59

$1.19	$1.22	$5.50	$14.40	$15.60	$4.70
- .65	- .96	+ 2.30	+ .77	- 6.90	+ 6.50

©2005 by Evan-Moor Corp. • Daily Summer Activities 3-4 • EMC 1030

Spell It!

Fill in each blank using the correct form of the word.

long	Jim ran for a _____ distance than Randy.
stir	Grandpa _____ his famous barbecue sauce.
study	The girls _____ for their tests last night.
swim	We were _____ in the lake when it began to rain.

Write your full name and address using your best handwriting.

_____

- -

_____

- -

_____

- -

_____

©2005 by Evan-Moor Corp. • Daily Summer Activities 3-4 • EMC 1030

Add **adjectives** to each sentence below. Make sure that the words you use make sense. There are many possible answers.

1. The elephant stood in the water.

   The _____ elephant stood in the _____ water.

2. Dr. Samson sat in a chair and read a book.

   Dr. Samson sat in the _____ chair and read the _____ book.

3. The ladies made quilts.

   The _____ ladies made _____ quilts.

Now think of additional adjectives that could be used for each sentence.

MATH TIME

Color the correct number of items to show each fraction.

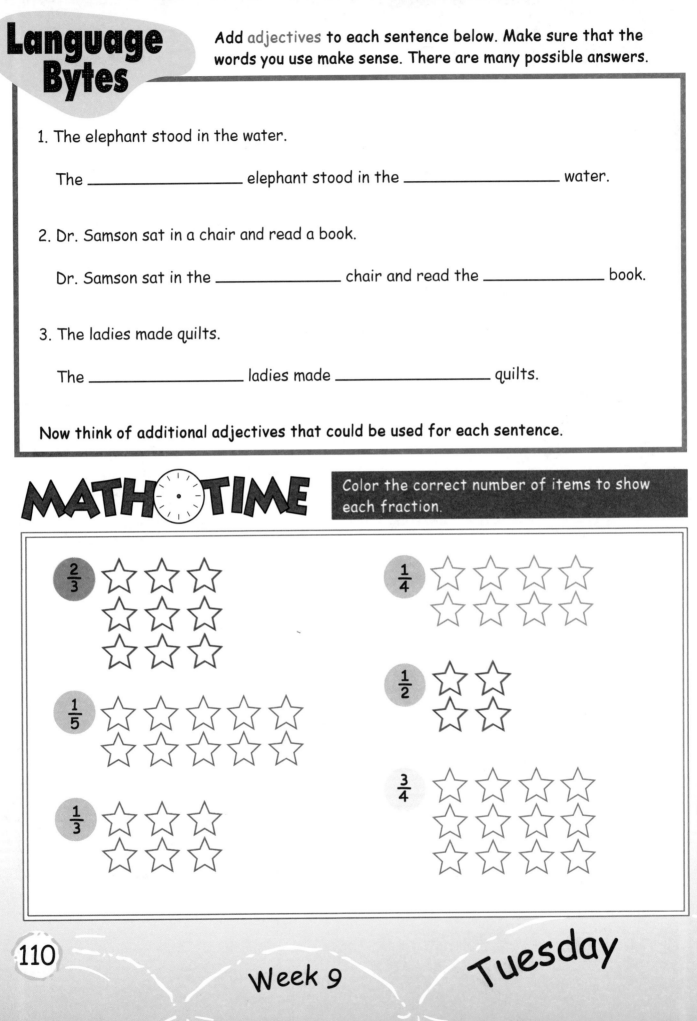

©2005 by Evan-Moor Corp. • Daily Summer Activities 3-4 • EMC-1030

Another Unnamed Story

Veterinarians are animal doctors. They go to school for many years. They learn all kinds of things about animals. They learn what foods animals need for good health. They learn about animal diseases and how to treat and prevent them.

Pet owners depend on veterinarians to help keep their pets healthy. Dogs and cats need regular vaccinations and checkups. They need the right kind and amount of food. They need regular exercise. And pets need love and attention. Veterinarians enjoy working with pet owners to make sure their pets have proper care. Veterinarians also take care of injured animals. They set broken bones, stitch up wounds, and perform surgeries of all kinds.

Some veterinarians do not work with cats and dogs. They specialize in large animals. They work with cows, horses, pigs, and sheep. Other veterinarians are experts in the care of reptiles or birds. Some veterinarians even work at zoos.

Being a veterinarian is a difficult job. It requires a great deal of patience, hard work, and skill. Someone who loves animals can find it to be a very rewarding job.

1. List at least three things that pets need to stay healthy and happy.

   _____

   _____

2. A good title for this story would be
   a. How to Care for Your Pet   b. Animal Doctors   c. Working with Animals

3. What does *expert* mean?

   _____

Wednesday

Week 9

Look up the words below in a dictionary. Read the definition of each word. Then draw a picture to illustrate each definition.

jetty	scroll

MATH TIME

Fill in each blank using one of the numbers in the box. Use each number only once.

$$2 \quad 3 \quad 4 \quad 5$$

40 x _____
is between 100 and 150.

90 x _____
is between 150 and 200.

65 x _____
is between 200 and 300.

72 x _____
is between 300 and 400.

©2005 by Evan-Moor Corp. • Daily Summer Activities 3-4 • EMC 1030

Ge‑graphy

Draw a map of your house or apartment. Imagine that you have removed the roof and are flying overhead, looking down. Label each room.

In My Own Words

Which room in your house do you like best? Write a paragraph describing that room. Be sure to include details about the things that make that room a special place.

_____

_____

_____

_____

_____

MATH⊙TIME

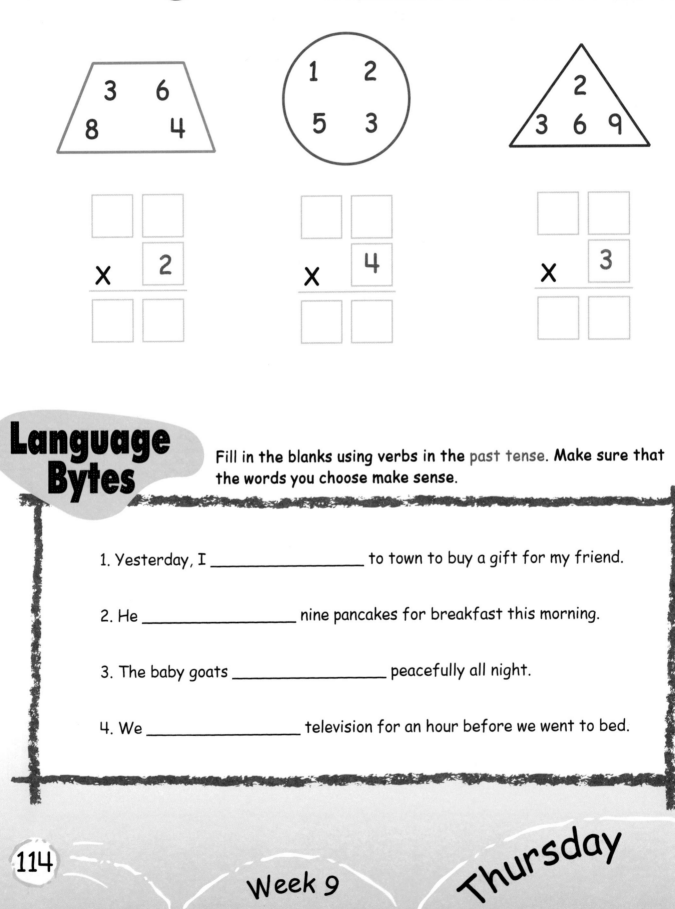

Language Bytes

Fill in the blanks using verbs in the past tense. Make sure that the words you choose make sense.

1. Yesterday, I _____ to town to buy a gift for my friend.

2. He _____ nine pancakes for breakfast this morning.

3. The baby goats _____ peacefully all night.

4. We _____ television for an hour before we went to bed.

Week 9

Thursday

Combine each pair of sentences to make one sentence.

1. Barbara went to the meeting. I went to the meeting.

   _____

   _____

2. Ken likes strawberries. Angie likes watermelon.

   _____

   _____

3. Put on your shoes. Put on your jacket.

   _____

MATH TIME

Complete each drawing. Each finished drawing should be symmetrical.

Friday

Week 9

A Hidden Picture

In the scene below, find the following hidden pictures:

ice-cream cone, sock, ring, crown, toothbrush, fish, hand, umbrella, ball, cup, and lamp.

©2005 by Evan-Moor Corp. • Daily Summer Activities 3-4 • EMC 1030

Color a ⭐ for each page finished.

Parent's Initials

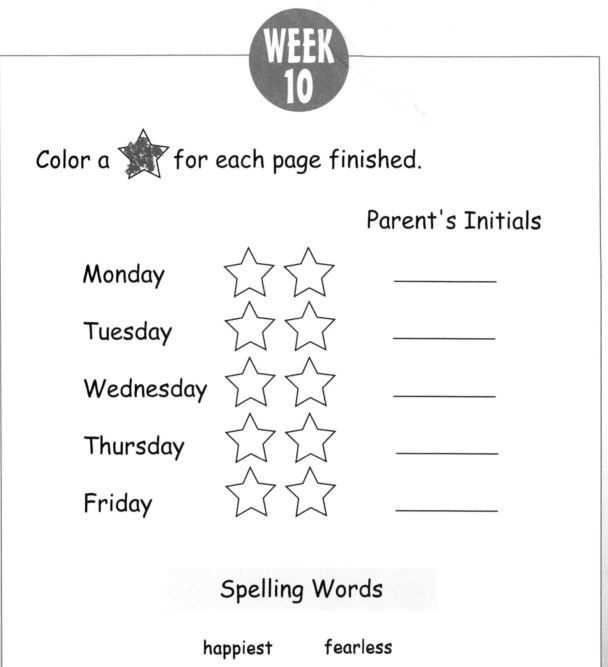

Monday

Tuesday

Wednesday

Thursday

Friday

_____

_____

_____

_____

_____

Spelling Words

happiest	fearless
wonderful	beautiful
strongest	careful
thoughtless	funniest
fastest	useful

A Memorable Moment

What sticks in your mind about this week?
Write about it.

_____

_____

_____

_____

Keeping Track

Color a book for every 15 minutes you read.

| Monday | Tuesday | Wednesday | Thursday | Friday |

Could the events in the book you are reading really happen?
Explain.

_____

_____

_____

_____

Questions and Answers

Question: _____

Answer: He likes his hamburger with ketchup, pickles, and tomatoes.

Question: _____

Answer: She is eleven years old.

Question: _____

Answer: The school fair will be held on the first Saturday in October.

Question: _____

Answer: Natasha has eleven dollars.

Question: _____

Answer: Rupert had a peanut butter and jelly sandwich and an apple.

Question: _____

Answer: The boys set up their tents, took a hike, and cooked dinner.

Now write your own question and answer it.

Question:

_____

Answer:

_____

Write It Right

1. wear your read dress to the mozart concert said mother

_____

_____

2. ive got an older brother and a younger sister

_____

_____

3. when you get home tell mike i have went to florida

_____

_____

MATH TIME

Find the answers.

329	211	136	199	287	306
- 146	- 54	+ 242	- 98	- 129	- 142

185	257	340	175	127	169
+ 216	+ 169	- 270	+ 84	+ 127	+ 352

©2005 by Evan-Moor Corp. • Daily Summer Activities 3-4 • EMC 1030

Spell It!

Write a word that means the opposite of each word below.

fastest _____

beautiful _____

strongest _____

careful _____

happiest _____

Write this sentence using your best handwriting.

Jake opened the gigantic yellow box and found a marvelous quetzal inside.

_____
_____
_____
_____
_____

What is a *quetzal*? Use a dictionary or an encyclopedia to find out. Draw a picture of a quetzal.

Language Bytes

If the guide words on a dictionary page were *hair* and *hamper*, which of the following words would not appear on that page? Cross off each word that would not appear.

hair		hamper
half		habit
handle		hammer
halo		hall
haunt		halibut
hale		hail

MATH TIME

Use a ruler to measure each object.

Measure to the nearest half inch.

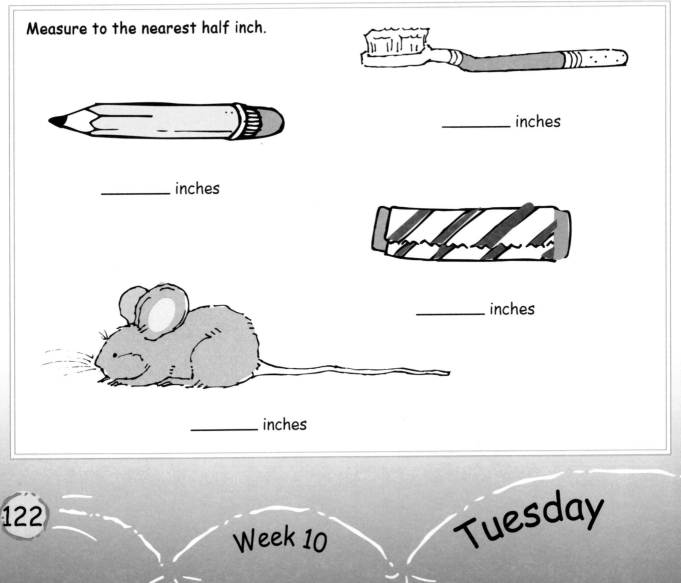

_____ inches

_____ inches

_____ inches

_____ inches

Below are directions for baking a cake, but they are all mixed up! Number the sentences from 1 to 9 to put the directions in the order that makes sense. Draw a line through the one sentence that does <u>not</u> belong with the others.

How to Bake a Cake

_____ Pour the batter into the cake pans.

_____ Mix the ingredients together according to the recipe.

_____ Allow the cake to cool.

_____ Spread frosting over the top and sides of the cake.

_____ Wash your hands.

_____ Chop two large onions.

_____ Read the recipe to make sure you have all the ingredients.

_____ Place the cake in the oven to bake.

_____ Remove the cake from the oven.

_____ Measure all ingredients carefully.

What is your favorite kind of cake?

_____

Language Bytes

Complete each sentence using an adjective and an adverb. Make sure that the words you use make sense. There are many possible answers.

1. The bear walked into the woods.

   The _____ bear walked _____ into the woods.

2. The girl wrapped the package.

   The _____ girl _____ wrapped the package.

3. The teacher spoke to the class.

   The _____ teacher spoke _____ to the class.

MATH TIME

Find the answers.

1. Rudy has a pizza parlor. On Friday, he sold 114 pepperoni pizzas, 98 cheese pizzas, and 49 mushroom pizzas. How many pizzas did he sell on Friday?

   _____

2. On Saturday, Rudy sold 22 more pepperoni pizzas than he did on Friday. He also sold 62 mushroom pizzas and 97 cheese pizzas. How many pepperoni pizzas did he sell on Saturday?

   _____

3. How many pizzas did Rudy sell on Friday and Saturday together?

   _____

©2005 by Evan-Moor Corp. • Daily Summer Activities 3-4 • EMC 1030

Geography

Draw a map showing how to get from your home to a place you can walk to. This might be a friend's house, a park, or a store. Label each street.

In My Own Words

Make a list of at least five words that can be used in place of the word said. Use three of the words in a sentence.

321	65	135	25	100	71
x 2	x 6	x 5	x 3	x 30	x 6

246	19	159	280	76	200
x 2	x 3	x 3	x 2	x 4	x 40

Language Bytes

Draw a circle around each word below that is a kind of plant. You may need to use a dictionary.

cypress	phlox	periwinkle	sickle	blubber
nettle	retina	hickory	gentian	flax

Language Bytes

Fill in each blank using a group of words that gives more information about the underlined word.

1. Our family has <u>pets</u>.

   Our family has _____.

2. Lenny keeps his <u>toys</u> on the shelf.

   Lenny keeps his _____ on the shelf.

3. Anna plays several <u>sports</u>.

   Anna plays _____.

MATH TIME

Find the answers.

This graph shows the number of students in each grade at Topanga Elementary School. Use the information on the graph to answer the questions.

Which grade has the most students?

_____

Which grade has the fewest students?

_____

Which three grades combined equal half of the student body?

_____

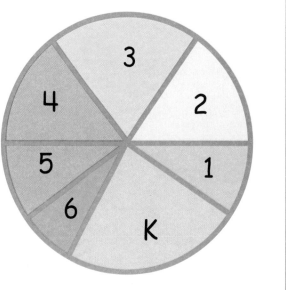

Australian Friend

B2 D5 A4 D4 B1 B5 A6 C3

B3 A2 B4 D3 A5 C6 D1 C2

C4 A3 D2 C5 B6 D6 A1 C1

Copy the lines in each box above in the correct place on the grid to find a friend from the land down under, Australia.

Week 10

Friday

Hooray for Me!

I finished my summer practice book. Now I'm ready for 4th grade!

name

date

Answer Key

Checking your child's work is an important part of learning. It allows you to see what your child knows well and what areas need more practice. It also provides an opportunity for you to help your child understand that making mistakes is a part of learning.

When an error is discovered, ask your child to look carefully at the question or problem. Errors often occur through misreading the problem. Your child can quickly correct these errors.

The answer key pages can be used in several ways:

- Remove the answer pages and give the book to your child. Go over the answers with him or her as each day's work is completed.

- Leave the answer pages in the book and give the practice pages to your child one day at a time.

- Leave the answer pages in the book so your child can check his or her own answers as the pages are completed. It is still important that you review the pages with your child if you use this method.

Page 11

Page 12

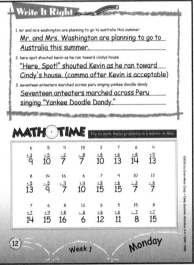

Page 13

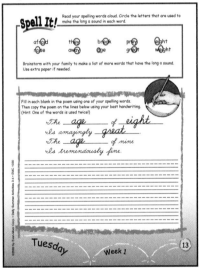

Page 14

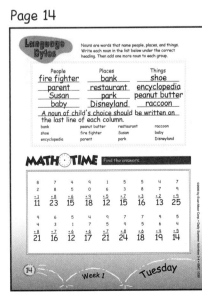

Page 15

Page 16

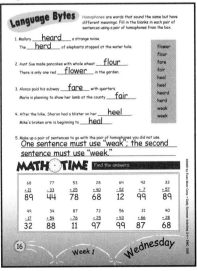

Page 17

Geography

Use an atlas or a globe.

Find the continent of North America. Color it red.

Write an X on South America.

Color Africa green.

Label the Pacific Ocean and the Atlantic Ocean.

Color all the oceans blue.

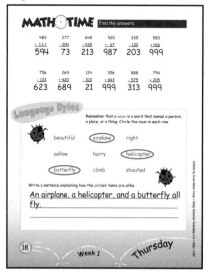

Write a List

Make a list of four fun things to do on Saturdays.
1. Answers will vary.
2. _____
3. _____
4. _____

Write a sentence or two telling which of these things you like best and why.

_____

Thursday Week 1 (17)

Page 18

MATH TIME Find the answers.

483	277	648	920	335	583
+ 111	- 204	- 435	+ 67	- 132	+ 416
594	73	213	987	203	999

756	269	124	356	888	794
- 133	+ 420	- 103	+ 643	- 575	+ 205
623	689	21	999	313	999

Language Bytes

Remember that a noun is a word that names a person, a place, or a thing. Circle the noun in each row.

beautiful   (airplane)   right

yellow   hurry   (helicopter)

(butterfly)   climb   shouted

Write a sentence explaining how the circled items are alike.

An airplane, a helicopter, and a butterfly all fly.

(18) Week 1 Thursday

Page 19

Language Bytes

Write the name of each fruit on the line next to its picture.

Write your list again, this time in alphabetical order.

pineapple	banana
banana	orange
pear	pear
strawberry	pineapple
orange	strawberry

MATH TIME Find the answers.

1. Shirley collected seashells on her vacation at the seashore. On Sunday she found 3 conch shells. On Monday she found 7 alive shells. On Tuesday she found 9 scallop shells. On Wednesday she found 8 whelk shells. How many seashells did Shirley find altogether?   **27 shells**

2. Fred earned $9.75 washing cars. He decided to spend some of the money on a movie ticket. If the movie ticket cost $3.50, how much money did Fred have left?   **$6.25 left**

3. Sandy has already finished reading two books on her summer reading list. The first book had 211 pages. The second book had 168 pages. How many pages has Sandy read altogether?   **379 pages**

Friday Week 1 (19)

Page 20

Who's Behind the Door?

If you knocked on each of these doors, who would answer? Draw a line from each door to the character that would most likely answer your knock.

What would each character say? Write a response for each character in the speech bubble.

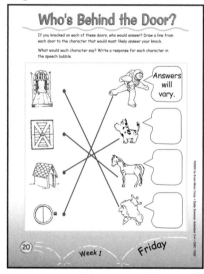

Answers will vary.

(20) Week 1 Friday

Page 23

Please Make Sense

Find the nonsense word in each pair of sentences below. Replace that word in each sentence with the same real word. Make sure the word you choose makes sense in both of the sentences.

The carpenter uses a hammer to tumple the nails.
My mother bought a tumple of sugar.   **pound**

The coach told us to stand in a straight winging.
Mr. Hoover used clean paper to winging the shelves.   **line**

It is hard to be lammy when you are waiting for your turn.
The lammy in the hospital bed was feeling much better.   **patient**

Elliott threw a doodop to Beau, who then made a touchdown.
I hope that I doodop my math test.   **pass**

The neighbor's dog likes to gullybug all night.
The gullybug on a birch tree is smooth and white.   **bark**

Dad said, "Please use your puffit instead of your fingers."
When we came to the puffit in the road, we were not sure which way to go.   **fork**

Annie likes to keevil her baby sister to sleep.
Mark and his friend climbed to the top of a large keevil.   **rock**

Monday Week 2 (23)

Page 24

Write It Right

1. my fathers office is at 201 elmwood dr frankfurt kentucky
My father's office is at 201 Elmwood Dr. Frankfurt, Kentucky.

2. where is the baseball field
Where is the baseball field?

3. paul and janet have invited us over to there house
Paul and Janet have invited us over to their house.

MATH TIME Find the answers. ★★

3	5	4	5	8	3	7
x 4	x 2	x 3	x 4	x 8	x 9	x 2
12	10	12	20	56	27	14

5	3	4	9	5	6	6
x 8	x 7	x 6	x 4	x 7	x 8	x 3
40	21	24	36	35	48	18

9	4	8	8	9	5	9
x 9	x 7	x 3	x 8	x 7	x 5	x 2
81	28	24	64	63	25	18

(24) Week 2 Monday

Page 25

Spell It! Answer these questions using your spelling words.

1. Which word means "very, very small"?   tiny
2. Which word means "an open, grassy area"?   field
3. What is the opposite of dirty?   clean
4. What do you call one part of a puzzle, or one slice of a pie?   piece
5. Which word means "at last"?   finally
6. Which word do you use when you are asking someone to give you something?   please
7. What is the opposite of sent?   received

Fill in the blanks in the sentences below using your spelling words. Then copy the sentences using your best handwriting.

While the giant slept. Jack crept **quietly** out of the cupboard. He tried to be **silent**.

_____

These sentences are part of a familiar story. What is the name of the story?
Jack and the Beanstalk

Tuesday Week 2 (25)

Page 26

Language Bytes

Plurals are nouns that mean "more than one." Match each noun on the left to its plural on the right.

child	bananas
tree	geese
goose	girls
class	children
leaf	trees
banana	classes
boy	leaves
girl	boys

Notice that plurals are formed in several different ways. Which way of forming plurals is used most often?
add "s"

MATH TIME Find the answers.

9	6	8	6	9	4	9
x 8	x 7	x 8	x 6	x 5	x 8	x 2
72	42	64	36	45	32	18

6	8	5	3	7	6	5
x 5	x 7	x 3	x 8	x 7	x 3	x 4
30	56	15	24	49	18	20

3	6	7	4	7	8	9
x 4	x 9	x 2	x 4	x 6	x 2	x 4
12	54	14	16	42	16	36

(26) Week 2 Tuesday

Page 27

A Wonder of the Sea

The octopus is an odd-looking animal that lives in the ocean. It has a soft body that is covered with a tough membrane called a *mantle*. It has eight long arms called *tentacles*. The tentacles are lined with strong muscles that act like suction cups. The octopus uses these tentacles to crack open the shells of clams and crabs. It then uses its sharp beak to eat the meat of the shellfish.

The octopus has a very interesting and unusual body. It has large bright eyes that can see quite well. Like fish, it uses gills to breathe underwater. The octopus has three hearts. The octopus moves by drawing water into its body and then quickly forcing the water out. This force propels the octopus backward through the water. The octopus can shoot an inky liquid out of its body. This liquid forms a cloud in the water and helps hide the octopus from sharks and other animals that might try to eat it. The octopus can also hide by changing colors to blend with its surroundings. When the octopus is excited, it can turn bright colors such as red, purple, or blue.

Octopuses come in many sizes. The smallest octopuses are only a few inches across. The largest may reach nearly 30 feet when measured across its outstretched tentacles. The octopus may look scary, but it rarely attacks people.

The octopus is truly one of the wonders of the sea.

1. What are tentacles?   long arms
2. What is a mantle?   a tough outer membrane
3. What does the octopus eat?   clams, crabs
4. List two ways the octopus can hide from danger   changes colors; shoots a cloud of dark ink
5. Why does the author call the octopus a "wonder of the sea"?
An octopus is interesting and unusual.

Wednesday Week 2 (27)

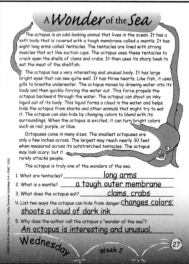

Page 28

Language Bytes

Write the plural of each word in the blank. You will need to make spelling changes in some of the words.

1. Sarah could not find her car **keys**.
   key
2. The **families** gathered for a neighborhood party.
   family
3. Seven **elves** danced around the fire.
   elf
4. The waiter served six **glasses** of ice water.
   glass
5. The **children** had fun at the circus.
   child
6. Mrs. Soldowski has four **rabbits**.
   rabbit

MATH TIME — Find the answers.

36 +29 = **65**	94 +48 = **142**	57 -34 = **23**	66 +91 = **157**	75 -25 = **50**	63 +38 = **101**	94 -73 = **21**
84 +58 = **142**	69 -42 = **27**	78 +88 = **166**	32 +59 = **91**	43 +64 = **107**	88 -54 = **34**	65 -21 = **44**

(28) Week 2 Wednesday

Page 29

Geography

Use an atlas, a globe, or a map of the United States to find the name of each numbered body of water.

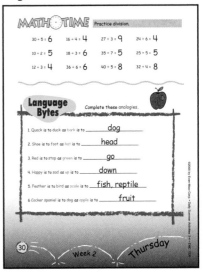

1. Pacific Ocean
2. Atlantic Ocean
3. Mississippi River
4. Lake Superior
5. Lake Michigan
6. Lake Huron
7. Lake Erie
8. Lake Ontario

In My Own Words

Read the paragraph below and then write a topic sentence that could begin the paragraph.

Sentences will vary. _____

Mr. and Mrs. Smith play tennis or golf almost every day. Buddy Smith is on the football team at the high school. Sissy Smith is a star forward on the soccer team at the park. The Smiths all enjoy swimming and running on the weekends.

Thursday Week 2 (29)

Page 30

MATH TIME — Practice division.

30 ÷ 5 = **6**	16 ÷ 4 = **4**	27 ÷ 3 = **9**	24 ÷ 6 = **4**
10 ÷ 2 = **5**	18 ÷ 3 = **6**	35 ÷ 7 = **5**	25 ÷ 5 = **5**
12 ÷ 3 = **4**	36 ÷ 6 = **6**	40 ÷ 5 = **8**	32 ÷ 4 = **8**

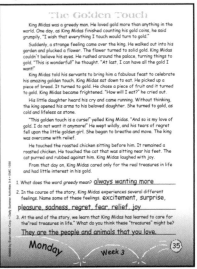

Language Bytes — Complete these analogies.

1. Quack is to duck as bark is to **dog**
2. Shoe is to foot as hat is to **head**
3. Red is to stop as green is to **go**
4. Happy is to sad as up is to **down**
5. Feather is to bird as scale is to **fish, reptile**
6. Cocker spaniel is to dog as apple is to **fruit**

(30) Week 2 Thursday

Page 31

Language Bytes

Synonyms are words that mean the same thing. Write a synonym for the underlined word in each sentence.

1. My grandmother has a little dog named Toby. **tiny, small, wee**
2. I had a terrible headache yesterday. **awful, horrible**
3. Lynne was glad to see her friend. **happy, pleased**

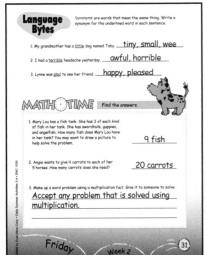

MATH TIME — Find the answers.

1. Mary Lou has a fish tank. She has 3 of each kind of fish in her tank. She has swordtails, guppies, and angelfish. How many fish does Mary Lou have in her tank? You may want to draw a picture to help solve the problem.   **9 fish**

2. Angie wants to give 4 carrots to each of her 5 horses. How many carrots does she need?   **20 carrots**

3. Make up a word problem using a multiplication fact. Give it to someone to solve.
Accept any problem that is solved using multiplication.

Friday Week 2 (31)

Page 32

Two boys, Kirt and Andrew, and three girls, Doris, Gail, and Barbara, went out to dinner. Each one in the group ordered a different meal. Read the clues below to find out where each person sat and what each had for dinner. Write your answers on the lines.

Doris sat between Gail and the boy who had a burrito.
The girl who had pizza was not Barbara.
Andrew sat next to the girl who had fried chicken.
The girl who had fried chicken sat in chair #4.
The boy who had spaghetti sat between Barbara and Kirt.
Gail had a hamburger.
Kirt sat in chair #1.

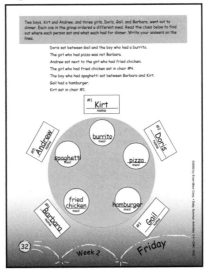

(32) Week 2 Friday

Page 35

The Golden Touch

King Midas was a greedy man. He loved gold more than anything in the world. One day, as King Midas finished counting his gold coins, he said grumpily, "I wish that everything I touch would turn to gold."

Suddenly, a strange feeling came over the king. He walked out into his garden and plucked a flower. The flower turned to solid gold. King Midas couldn't believe his eyes. He rushed around the palace, turning things to gold. "This is wonderful!" he thought. "At last, I can have all the gold I want!"

King Midas told his servants to bring him a fabulous feast to celebrate his amazing golden touch. King Midas sat down to eat. He picked up a piece of bread. It turned to gold. He chose a piece of fruit and it turned to gold. King Midas became frightened. "How will I eat?" he cried out.

His little daughter heard his cry and came running. Without thinking, the king opened his arms to his beloved daughter. She turned to gold, as cold and lifeless as stone.

"This golden touch is a curse!" yelled King Midas. "And so is my love of gold. I do not want it anymore!" He wept wildly, and his tears of regret fell upon the little golden girl. She began to breathe and move. The king was overcome with relief.

He touched the roasted chicken sitting before him. It remained a roasted chicken. He touched the cat that was sitting near his feet. The cat purred and rubbed against him. King Midas laughed with joy.

From that day on, King Midas cared only for the real treasures in life and had little interest in his gold.

1. What does the word greedy mean? **always wanting more**
2. In the course of the story, King Midas experiences several different feelings. Name some of these feelings. **excitement, surprise, pleasure, sadness, regret, fear, relief, joy**
3. At the end of the story, we learn that King Midas has learned to care for the "real treasures in life." What do you think these "treasures" might be? **They are the people and animals that you love.**

Monday Week 3 (35)

Page 36

Write It Right

1. are you going to eat that there doughnut
   Are you going to eat that doughnut?
2. mom would you buy some gum for julie and I
   Mom, would you buy some gum for Julie and me?
3. maria said I would like to go to
   Maria said, "I would like to go too."
   (Note: a comma before too is acceptable)

MATH TIME — Find the answers.

6 × 7 = **42**	9 × 5 = **45**	15 ÷ 3 = **5**	32 ÷ 4 = **8**
9 ÷ 3 = **3**	42 ÷ 6 = **7**	9 × 4 = **36**	45 ÷ 5 = **9**
8 × 4 = **32**	28 ÷ 7 = **4**	6 × 6 = **36**	5 × 7 = **35**
18 ÷ 2 = **9**	6 × 9 = **54**	21 ÷ 3 = **7**	8 × 8 = **64**
4 × 7 = **28**	7 × 6 = **42**	36 ÷ 6 = **6**	27 ÷ 3 = **9**

(36) Week 3 Monday

Page 37

Spell It!

All of this week's spelling words contain the long o sound. Fill in each blank below with a letter or combination of letters to make some additional long o words.

 bone

b **oa** st   m **oa** n   m **o** st

th **o** se   l **o** ne   h **o** me

v **o** te   h **o** le   thr **oa** t

Underline each word that contains the long o sound in the sentences below. Then copy the sentences using your best handwriting.

The clown joked about his funny clothes.

Do you know how to sew?

Tuesday Week 3 (37)

Page 38

Language Bytes

Adjectives are words that describe people, places, and things. An adjective can tell how something looks. It can tell what color, what kind, or how many.

Match each phrase with its picture. Then circle each adjective.

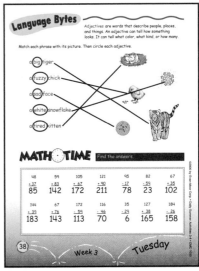

a **big** tiger
a **fuzzy** chick
a **sad** face
a **white** snowflake
a **tired** kitten

MATH TIME — Find the answers.

48 +37 = **85**	59 +83 = **142**	105 +67 = **172**	121 +90 = **211**	95 -17 = **78**	82 -59 = **23**	67 +35 = **102**
144 +39 = **183**	67 +76 = **143**	172 -59 = **113**	116 -46 = **70**	35 -29 = **6**	127 +38 = **165**	184 -26 = **158**

(38) Week 3 Tuesday

Another Unnamed Story

Salt is a mineral that forms in the earth. The kind of salt that is dug out of salt mines is actually a rock called *halite*. So every time you use a salt shaker, you are sprinkling tiny rocks on your food! Salt can also be evaporated from seawater. This method leaves a very pure salt that many people prefer because of its good taste.

Salt not only makes food taste good, it is very important to our health. Body cells need salt to stay alive. In fact, salt makes up almost one percent of our blood and cells. Animals need salt too. Farmers often put blocks of salt in the fields for animals to lick.

Salt has many other uses. Salt has long been used in preserving foods because it is antiseptic, or germ-killing. Salt is also used in making glass, soap, and other products.

In Poland there are some very famous and unusual salt mines. Here, for hundreds of years, miners have dug salt from deep beneath the earth's surface. They have carved elegant rooms and beautiful statues from the solid salt. Tourists visit the salt mines to view the salt statues.

Long ago, salt was valued very highly because it was important and hard to get. In many parts of the world today, salt is still prized as a symbol of purity and friendship.

1. A good title for this story is
   a. Farm Animals   **c. The Story of Salt**
   b. Rocks and Minerals   d. Making Food Taste Good

2. The word *antiseptic* means **germ-killing**

3. Name three important uses for salt.
Makes food taste good; needed by body cells; preserves food; used in making glass, soap, and other products.

Wednesday   Week 3   (39)

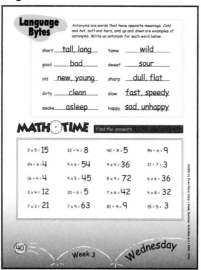

Language Bytes

Antonyms are words that have opposite meanings. *Cold* and *hot*, *soft* and *hard*, and *up* and *down* are examples of antonyms. Write an antonym for each word below.

short	**tall, long**	tame	**wild**
good	**bad**	sweet	**sour**
old	**new, young**	sharp	**dull, flat**
dirty	**clean**	slow	**fast, speedy**
awake	**asleep**	happy	**sad, unhappy**

MATH TIME — Find the answers.

3 × 5 = 15	32 ÷ 4 = 8	40 ÷ 8 = 5	54 ÷ 6 = 9
24 ÷ 6 = 4	9 × 6 = 54	9 × 4 = 36	21 ÷ 7 = 3
16 ÷ 4 = 4	9 × 5 = 45	8 × 9 = 72	6 × 6 = 36
3 × 4 = 12	30 ÷ 6 = 5	7 × 6 = 42	4 × 8 = 32
7 × 3 = 21	7 × 9 = 63	81 ÷ 9 = 9	15 ÷ 5 = 3

(40)   Week 3   Wednesday

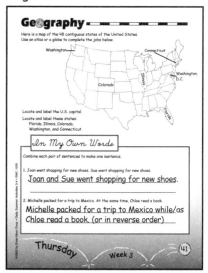

Geography

Here is a map of the 48 contiguous states of the United States. Use an atlas or a globe to complete the jobs below.

Washington — Connecticut — Illinois — Colorado — Washington, D.C. — Florida

Locate and label the U.S. capital.

Locate and label these states:
Florida, Illinois, Colorado, Washington, and Connecticut.

In My Own Words

Combine each pair of sentences to make one sentence.

1. Joan went shopping for new shoes. Sue went shopping for new shoes.
Joan and Sue went shopping for new shoes.

2. Michelle packed for a trip to Mexico. At the same time, Chloe read a book.
Michelle packed for a trip to Mexico while/as Chloe read a book. (or in reverse order)

Thursday   Week 3   (41)

MATH TIME — Find the answers.

12 × 3 = 36	10 × 5 = 50	20 × 2 = 40	22 × 4 = 88	11 × 6 = 66	31 × 3 = 93	22 × 4 = 88
43 × 2 = 86	11 × 9 = 99	23 × 3 = 69	10 × 8 = 80	20 × 3 = 60	14 × 2 = 28	30 × 2 = 60

Language Bytes

Rhyming words have the same ending sound. List at least three rhyming words for each word below.

Accept any rhyming word. Spellings may differ.

bead **could be ead or eed words**

gate **could be ate, ait, eight, or eat words**

hill _____

Make up a poem using some or all of your rhyming words.

Accept any 2-, 3-, or 4-line poem that rhymes.

(42)   Week 3   Thursday

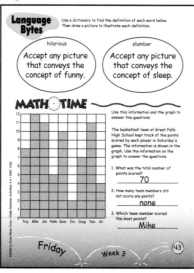

Language Bytes

Use a dictionary to find the definition of each word below. Then draw a picture to illustrate each definition.

hilarious — **Accept any picture that conveys the concept of funny.**

slumber — **Accept any picture that conveys the concept of sleep.**

MATH TIME

Use this information and the graph to answer the questions.

The basketball team of Great Falls High School kept track of the points scored by each player in Saturday's game. The information is shown in the graph. Use the information on the graph to answer the questions.

1. What was the total number of points scored?
70

2. How many team members did not score any points?
none

3. Which team member scored the most points?
Mike

Troy Mike Jim Pablo Gene Eric Doug Tran Ari

Friday   Week 3   (43)

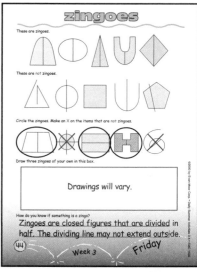

zingoes

These are zingoes.

These are not zingoes.

Circle the zingoes. Make an X on the items that are not zingoes.

Draw three zingoes of your own in this box.

Drawings will vary.

How do you know if something is a zingo?
Zingoes are closed figures that are divided in half. The dividing line may not extend outside.

(44)   Week 3   Friday

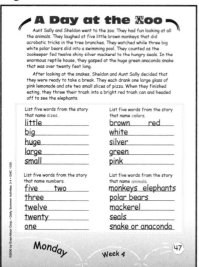

A Day at the Zoo

Aunt Sally and Sheldon went to the zoo. They had fun looking at all the animals. They laughed at five little brown monkeys that did acrobatic tricks in the tree branches. They watched while three big white polar bears slid into a swimming pool. They counted as the zookeeper fed twelve shiny silver mackerel to the hungry seals. In the enormous reptile house, they gasped at the huge green anaconda snake that was over twenty feet long.

After looking at the snakes, Sheldon and Aunt Sally decided that they were ready to take a break. They each drank one large glass of pink lemonade and ate two small slices of pizza. When they finished eating, they threw their trash into a bright red trash can and headed off to see the elephants.

List five words from the story that name sizes.	List five words from the story that name colors.
little	brown red
big	white
huge	silver
large	green
small	pink

List five words from the story that name numbers.	List five words from the story that name animals.
five two	monkeys elephants
three	polar bears
twelve	mackerel
twenty	seals
one	snake or anaconda

Monday   Week 4   (47)

Write It Right

1. our dad dont like to watch television
Our dad doesn't like to watch television.

2. the school bus arrives at sandpoint school at 810 in the morning
The school bus arrives at Sandpoint School at 8:10 in the morning.

3. theirs a fire in the building
There's a fire in the building!

MATH TIME — Find the answers.

48 − 19 = 29	65 + 37 = 102	57 + 94 = 151	83 − 65 = 18	104 − 28 = 76	56 + 29 = 85	66 + 46 = 112
77 + 43 = 120	91 − 28 = 63	44 + 39 = 83	132 − 46 = 86	125 + 55 = 180	92 − 38 = 54	147 + 49 = 196
123 − 64 = 59	104 + 28 = 132	45 + 38 = 83	38 + 56 = 94	75 − 49 = 26	136 − 87 = 49	108 − 68 = 40

(48)   Week 4   Monday

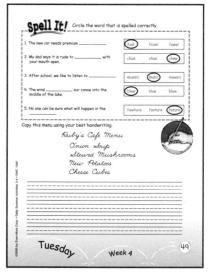

Spell It!

Circle the word that is spelled correctly.

1. The new car needs premium _____
   (fuel) fossel fewel

2. My dad says it is rude to _____ with your mouth open.
   choo chuw **(chew)**

3. After school, we like to listen to _____
   muesic **(music)** mewsic

4. The wind _____ our canoe into the middle of the lake.
   (blew) blue bluw

5. No one can be sure what will happen in the _____
   feature facture **(future)**

Copy this menu using your best handwriting.

Ruby's Cafe Menu
Onion Soup
Stewed Mushrooms
New Potatoes
Cheese Cubes

Tuesday   Week 4   (49)

Page 50

Language Bytes

Pronouns are words that take the place of nouns. Here are some pronouns that you already know:

she he it we they

Write the correct pronoun on each line.

1. Martin has a bicycle. **He** likes to ride **it**.

2. Roger and Emily made some gingerbread. **They** put whipped cream on **it**.

3. Elizabeth ran after the ball. **She** caught **it**.

MATH TIME — Find the answers.

16 ×4 = **64**	31 ×6 = **186**	52 ×3 = **156**	45 ×2 = **90**	63 ×5 = **315**	52 ×4 = **208**	63 ×6 = **378**
29 ×3 = **87**	72 ×2 = **144**	65 ×3 = **195**	94 ×2 = **188**	80 ×4 = **320**	21 ×6 = **126**	15 ×2 = **30**

50   Week 4   Tuesday

Page 51

★ ★ ★ John Glenn ★ ★ ★

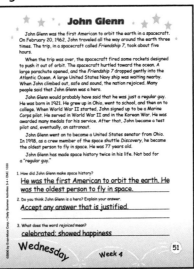

John Glenn was the first American to orbit the earth in a spacecraft. On February 20, 1962, John traveled all the way around the earth three times. The trip, in a spacecraft called *Friendship 7*, took about five hours.

When the trip was over, the spacecraft fired some rockets designed to push it out of orbit. The spacecraft hurtled toward the ocean. A large parachute opened, and the *Friendship 7* dropped gently into the Atlantic Ocean. A large United States Navy ship was waiting nearby. When John climbed out, safe and sound, the nation rejoiced. Many people said that John Glenn was a hero.

John Glenn would probably have said that he was just a regular guy. He was born in 1921. He grew up in Ohio, went to school, and then on to college. When World War II started, John signed up to be a Marine Corps pilot. He served in World War II and in the Korean War. He was awarded many medals for his service. After that, John became a test pilot and, eventually, an astronaut.

John Glenn went on to become a United States senator from Ohio. In 1998, as a crew member of the space shuttle *Discovery*, he became the oldest person to fly in space. He was 77 years old.

John Glenn has made space history twice in his life. Not bad for a "regular guy."

1. How did John Glenn make space history?
He was the first American to orbit the earth. He was the oldest person to fly in space.

2. Do you think John Glenn is a hero? Explain your answer.
Accept any answer that is justified.

3. What does the word *rejoiced* mean?
celebrated; showed happiness

Wednesday   Week 4   51

Page 52

Language Bytes

Replace the underlined word in each sentence with an antonym that makes more sense.

1. Jim lifts weights to make his muscles weak.
strong

2. Callie put on a sweater because the weather was so warm.
cold, cool

3. The hungry dog wanted less food to eat.
more

4. Brad put a pad under his sleeping bag because the ground was so soft.
hard

5. Our family eats lunch in the middle of the night.
day

MATH TIME — Find the answers.

1. Janice made bead necklaces to sell at the county fair. She worked for 30 days. She used 24 beads on each necklace. She made 6 necklaces each day.

How many beads did she use each day?   **144 beads**

How many necklaces did she make altogether?   **180 necklaces**

2. On the first day of the fair, Janice sold 52 necklaces for $3 each. How much money did she make that day?   **$156**

52   Week 4   Wednesday

Page 53

Geography

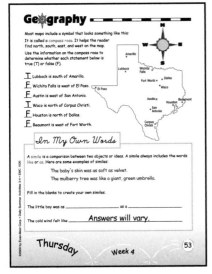

Most maps include a symbol that looks something like this. It is called a compass rose. It helps the reader find north, south, east, and west on the map.

Use the information on the compass rose to determine whether each statement below is true (T) or false (F).

T Lubbock is south of Amarillo.

F Wichita Falls is west of El Paso.

F Austin is west of San Antonio.

T Waco is north of Corpus Christi.

F Houston is north of Dallas.

F Beaumont is west of Fort Worth.

In My Own Words

A simile is a comparison between two objects or ideas. A simile always includes the words like or as. Here are some examples of similes:

The baby's skin was as soft as velvet.

The mulberry tree was like a giant, green umbrella.

Fill in the blanks to create your own similes.

The little boy was as _____ as a _____.

The cold wind felt like _____.

Answers will vary.

Thursday   Week 4   53

Page 54

MATH TIME — Find the answers.

18 ×5 = **90**	27 ×4 = **108**	69 ×2 = **138**	54 ×3 = **162**	71 ×3 = **213**	29 ×4 = **116**	13 ×5 = **65**
90 ×2 = **180**	62 ×5 = **310**	31 ×4 = **124**	78 ×3 = **234**	92 ×5 = **460**	40 ×3 = **120**	61 ×2 = **122**

Language Bytes

Circle each pair of words that are synonyms. Draw a line under each pair of words that are antonyms.

tight / loose

fast / slow

smooth / rough

(pretty / lovely)

hard / soft

(easy / simple)

awake / asleep

(moist / damp)

54   Week 4   Thursday

Page 55

Language Bytes

Some pronouns are used to show ownership.

my your his her its our their

Fill in the blanks using the possessive pronouns above.

Answers will vary.

1. Please put **your** litter in the trash can.

2. Serena and Jesse found **their** lost dog.

3. Candace wants **her** birthday party to be special.

4. I have lots of fun with **my** best friend.

MATH TIME — Pick an apple from the tree to complete each number sentence.

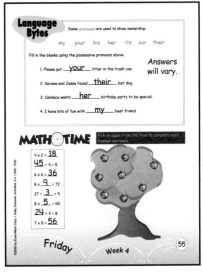

9 × 2 = **18**

45 ÷ 9 = **5**

6 × 6 = **36**

8 × **9** = 72

27 ÷ 3 = 9

8 × **5** = 40

24 ÷ **4** = 6

7 × 8 = **56**

Friday   Week 4   55

Page 56

Elf Twins

Two of the elves on this page are twins. They look exactly alike. Circle them.

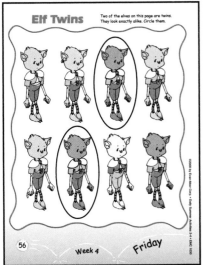

56   Week 4   Friday

Page 59

Growing Salad

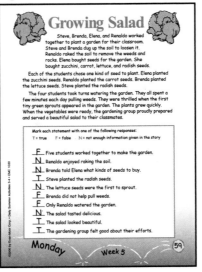

Steve, Brenda, Elena, and Renaldo worked together to plant a garden for their classroom. Steve and Brenda dug up the soil to loosen it. Renaldo raked the soil to remove the weeds and rocks. Elena bought seeds for the garden. She bought zucchini, carrot, lettuce, and radish seeds.

Each of the students chose one kind of seed to plant. Elena planted the zucchini seeds. Renaldo planted the carrot seeds. Brenda planted the lettuce seeds. Steve planted the radish seeds.

The four students took turns watering the garden. They all spent a few minutes each day pulling weeds. They were thrilled when the first tiny green sprouts appeared in the garden. The plants grew quickly. When the vegetables were ready, the gardening group proudly prepared and served a beautiful salad to their classmates.

Mark each statement with one of the following responses:

T = true   F = false   N = not enough information given in the story

F Five students worked together to make the garden.

N Renaldo enjoyed raking the soil.

N Brenda told Elena what kinds of seeds to buy.

T Steve planted the radish seeds.

N The lettuce seeds were the first to sprout.

F Brenda did not help pull weeds.

F Only Renaldo watered the garden.

N The salad tasted delicious.

T The salad looked beautiful.

T The gardening group felt good about their efforts.

Monday   Week 5   59

Page 60

Write It Right

1. last tuesday was warrens ninth birthday
Last Tuesday was Warren's ninth birthday.

2. in april samantha took the train to augusta maine
In April Samantha took a train to Augusta, Maine.

3. he seen the movie titanic with us
He saw the movie Titanic with us.

MATH TIME — Find the answers.

131 ×4 = **524**	200 ×6 = **1200**	122 ×7 = **854**	410 ×5 = **2050**	242 ×3 = **726**	55 ×4 = **220**
154 ×3 = **462**	165 ×2 = **330**	99 ×4 = **396**	116 ×3 = **348**	203 ×2 = **406**	150 ×5 = **750**

60   Week 5   Monday

Page 61

Spell It!
Write the spelling words that are formed from these sets of words.

cannot	can't	we are	we're
does not	doesn't	did not	didn't
I will	I'll	would not	wouldn't
do not	don't	will not	won't
let us	let's	are not	aren't

Copy the following sentences using your best handwriting.

A contraction combines two words into one. An apostrophe is placed in the contraction to show that a letter or letters are missing.

Tuesday   Week 5   61

Page 62

Language Bytes
Verbs are words that show action. Circle each word below that describes an action.

(run) (talk) book lamp (eat) (spin)
(dance) (sit) (jump) dog (catch) shirt
shoe (work) (write) (leap) orange (climb)

MATH TIME — Fill in the missing numbers.
Complete each number sentence, both vertically and horizontally.

48	÷	8	=	6
÷		✿		÷
6	÷	2	=	3
=		✿		=
8		4		2

62   Week 5   Tuesday

Page 63

Nocturnal Animals

Did you know that when you go to bed at night, many animals are just beginning to stir? These animals sleep during much of the day and come out at night to hunt for food. Animals who are active during the hours of darkness are called *nocturnal animals*. Owls, raccoons, skunks, moths, mice, and bats are just a few of these animals.

You might think that it would be difficult for nocturnal animals to find their way around in the dark, but it isn't. Some of them have eyes that are specially formed to make use of moonlight and starlight. Their eyes are almost like mirrors that magnify the light and enable them to see quite well. Other animals rely on their noses. Mice, for example, use their sense of smell to guide them to food sources. Some animals rely on their ears. An owl can hear the soft rustling sound made by a mouse as it slips through the grass.

Go outside on a summer evening and sit quietly. Perhaps you will see or hear some nocturnal animals. Listen for the chirp of crickets. Watch the sky for a bat swooping after mosquitoes. Look around a porch light for moths and other insects that may be attracted to the glow. You might discover that nighttime brings a lot of action to your very own backyard!

1. What does *nocturnal* mean?
   active during the night

2. Mice use their sense of _smell_ to help them find food.

3. List three nocturnal animals you might see near your home.
   Answers will vary.

Wednesday   Week 5   63

Page 64

Language Bytes
Make a list of at least four adjectives that describe the animal in the picture below.

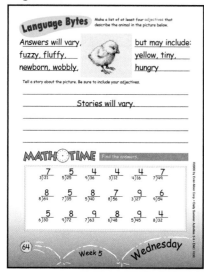

Answers will vary, but may include:
fuzzy, fluffy, yellow, tiny,
newborn, wobbly, hungry

Tell a story about the picture. Be sure to include your adjectives.

Stories will vary.

MATH TIME — Find the answers.

7	5	4	4	4	7
3)21	5)25	9)36	3)12	4)16	7)44
8	7	5	8	9	6
8)64	7)35	9)40	8)56	9)27	9)54
5	8	9	8	9	4
6)30	9)72	7)63	6)48	5)45	8)32

64   Week 5   Wednesday

Page 65

Geography

The scale of the map lets the reader know how much real distance is represented on map.

Use the scale shown below to answer the questions. Use a ruler or estimate your answers.

About how far is it from Waterville to Brunswick?
50 miles

About how far is it from Lewiston to Augusta?
25 miles

About how far is it from Portland to Skowhegan?
100 miles

Scale: ½ inch = 25 miles

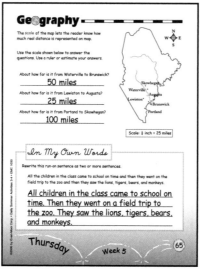

In My Own Words

Rewrite this run-on sentence as two or more sentences.

All the children in the class came to school on time and then they went on the field trip to the zoo and then they saw the lions, tigers, bears, and monkeys.

All children in the class came to school on time. Then they went on a field trip to the zoo. They saw the lions, tigers, bears, and monkeys.

Thursday   Week 5   65

Page 66

MATH TIME — Round these numbers to the nearest 10.

57	60	42	40	16	20
88	90	95	100	23	20
169	170	204	200	131	130

Language Bytes

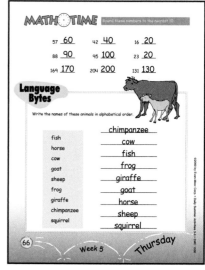

Write the names of these animals in alphabetical order.

fish	chimpanzee
horse	cow
cow	fish
goat	frog
sheep	giraffe
frog	goat
giraffe	horse
chimpanzee	sheep
squirrel	squirrel

66   Week 5   Thursday

Page 67

Spell It!
Fill in each blank below using any verb that makes sense in the sentence. Try to make your verbs "colorful." For example, instead of *ate*, you might choose *gobbled*.

Answers will vary.

1. The baby likes to _____ across the carpet.
2. The mouse _____ away from the cat.
3. Joe and Carol went to the lake to _____ in the water.
4. Mac knows how to _____ the basketball.
5. The horse _____ across the meadow.

MATH TIME — Find the answers.

1. Selena's father made cookies for a class party. He made 3 cookies for each student in the class. He made 75 cookies altogether. How many students are in Selena's class?
   25 students

2. Cans of lemonade are on sale at Dailey's Market at 2 cans for 88¢. What is the cost of one can of lemonade?
   44¢ for one can

3. Benny the baker is making a wedding cake. The cake is going to have 5 layers. He needs 12 eggs for each layer. How many eggs does he need?
   60 eggs

Friday   Week 5   67

Page 68

Forest Maze
Help the lost hiker find his way through the forest and back to his tent.

68   Week 5   Friday

Page 71

Can you create a story?

Number the parts of this story in order from 1 to 9 to make a sensible story.

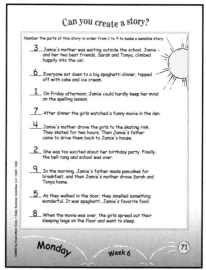

3 Jamie's mother was waiting outside the school. Jamie and her two best friends, Sarah and Tonya, climbed happily into the car.

6 Everyone sat down to a big spaghetti dinner, topped off with cake and ice cream.

1 On Friday afternoon, Jamie could hardly keep her mind on the spelling lesson.

7 After dinner the girls watched a funny movie in the den.

4 Jamie's mother drove the girls to the skating rink. They skated for two hours. Then Jamie's father came to drive them back to Jamie's house.

2 She was too excited about her birthday party. Finally, the bell rang and school was over.

9 In the morning, Jamie's father made pancakes for breakfast, and then Jamie's mother drove Sarah and Tonya home.

5 As they walked in the door, they smelled something wonderful. It was spaghetti, Jamie's favorite food.

8 When the movie was over, the girls spread out their sleeping bags on the floor and went to sleep.

Monday   Week 6   71

Page 72

Write It Right

1. dont you want to climb mount johnson
Don't you want to climb Mount Johnson?

2. dr palmer has went to the hospital all ready
Dr. Palmer has gone/went to the hospital already.

3. ella sang a song called its a beautiful day
Ella sang a song called "It's a Beautiful Day."

MATH TIME — Find the answers.

$9R1$ $\quad$ $5R2$ $\quad$ $6R2$ $\quad$ $5R3$ $\quad$ $9R4$ $\quad$ $8R2$
$2)\overline{19}$ $\quad$ $3)\overline{17}$ $\quad$ $4)\overline{26}$ $\quad$ $5)\overline{28}$ $\quad$ $8)\overline{76}$ $\quad$ $4)\overline{34}$

$7R2$ $\quad$ $7R1$ $\quad$ $7R5$ $\quad$ $7R4$ $\quad$ $6R1$ $\quad$ $9R1$
$6)\overline{44}$ $\quad$ $9)\overline{64}$ $\quad$ $6)\overline{47}$ $\quad$ $5)\overline{39}$ $\quad$ $2)\overline{13}$ $\quad$ $5)\overline{46}$

72 — Week 6 — Monday

Page 73

Spell It!

Your spelling words this week are all compound words. Match each word on the left with a word on the right to make a spelling word.

with — body
my — be
every — come
butter — work
basket — out
home — thing
some — side
be — ball
may — fly
out — self

Circle the compound words used in this poem. Then copy the poem using your best handwriting.

The *sunflowers* waved in the summer breeze.
A *rainbow* painted the sky.
A *grasshopper* jumped from leaf to leaf.
And a *butterfly* floated by.

Tuesday — Week 6

Page 74

Language Bytes

Homophones are words that sound alike but are spelled differently and have different meanings.
Complete each pair of sentences using a pair of homophones.

1. The robber tried to **steal** the jewelry.
The bridge was built of **steel**.

2. I read a fairy **tale** to my niece.
The cat's **tail** twitches when she sees a mouse.

3. The belt fits around his **waist**.
My family is careful not to **waste** food.

MATH TIME — Find the answers.

$7R1$ $\quad$ $4R2$ $\quad$ $7R1$ $\quad$ $7R2$ $\quad$ $4R2$ $\quad$ $6R1$
$2)\overline{15}$ $\quad$ $3)\overline{14}$ $\quad$ $5)\overline{36}$ $\quad$ $7)\overline{51}$ $\quad$ $4)\overline{18}$ $\quad$ $9)\overline{55}$

$8R4$ $\quad$ $8R3$ $\quad$ $9R2$ $\quad$ $7R1$ $\quad$ $8R1$ $\quad$ $9R6$
$5)\overline{44}$ $\quad$ $4)\overline{35}$ $\quad$ $5)\overline{47}$ $\quad$ $3)\overline{22}$ $\quad$ $7)\overline{57}$ $\quad$ $8)\overline{78}$

74 — Week 6 — Tuesday

Page 75

Jane Goodall

When Jane Goodall was twenty-six years old, she began a great adventure. The year was 1960. Jane went to Africa on a special project. Her job was to learn everything she could about chimpanzees. She set up her camp on a game reserve. (A game reserve is an area that has been set aside as a place where animals can live freely and safely.)

Jane went out into the forest every day. She sat and watched the chimpanzees for hours at a time. She wrote down every detail of their behavior. She got to know the chimpanzees very well. After a time, they came to trust her and accept her as a friend.

Jane's work led to several new discoveries. She found that chimpanzees use tools to get food. She watched as they poked sticks into termite holes to gather insects to eat. She also learned that chimpanzees sometimes hunt small animals for meat. This was a big surprise. Scientists had always thought that chimpanzees ate only fruit and vegetation.

National Geographic has produced many films and articles about Jane Goodall's work. Jane has also written books about her experiences.

Jane Goodall has dedicated her life to helping expand humankind's knowledge and understanding of animals. She continues her work today through the Jane Goodall Institute. To learn more, contact the Jane Goodall Institute at P.O. Box 14890, Silver Spring, Maryland 20911-4890.

1. Why did Jane Goodall go to Africa?
She had a job to learn about chimpanzees.

2. What surprising discoveries did Jane make?
Chimpanzees use tools to get food.
Chimpanzees sometimes eat meat.

3. This article is mostly about Jane Goodall's
a. books b. friends c. work

Wednesday — Week 6 — 75

Page 76

Language Bytes

Verbs can have different forms. A verb in the present tense tells an action that happens now. A verb in the past tense tells about an action that already happened.

Match each present tense verb with its past tense verb.

run — sang
swim — laughed
play — slid
speak — hopped
laugh — ran
hop — spoke
sing — swam
slide — played

MATH TIME — Find the answers.

Fill in each blank using a unit of measurement that makes sense in the sentence.

1. I worked on my book report for 2 **hours** last night.
2. My father is 6 **feet** tall.
3. The distance to my grandmother's house is 50 **miles**
4. Jorge went to the store to buy a **quart/gallon** of milk and 5 **pounds** of sugar.
5. Mr. Fitch is 63 **years** old.
6. The package was 12 **inches** wide.
7. The recipe calls for 3 **cups** of flour.

Answers may vary.

76 — Week 6 — Wednesday

Page 77

Geography

Maps can give us all kinds of information. This map of China uses color to show the average amounts of rainfall in different parts of that country.

Use the information contained in the key. Circle the correct answers.

The northeast /southeast area of China receives the most rainfall.

Dark blue indicates the greatest/least amount of rainfall.

An average rainfall of 20 to 40 inches is represented by which color?
a. ▓ b. ░ c. ▢

Rainfall in China

Rainfall in Inches
more than 80
60–80
40–60
20–40
4–20
less than 4

In My Own Words

Write a paragraph explaining how to build a sand castle. Include some of these words: first, next, then, after that, finally.

Answers will vary.

Thursday — Week 6 — 77

Page 78

MATH TIME — Write the numbers in order from least to greatest.

1. 61 4 72 54 113 68
4 54 61 68 72 113

2. 210 221 219 235 232 227
210 219 221 227 232 235

3. 1873 1765 1921 1780 1836 1909
1765 1780 1836 1873 1909 1921

Language Bytes

Adjectives make writing more interesting.
Choose interesting adjectives to complete each sentence below. Make sure that the words you use make sense in the sentence.

1. The house had windows.
The _____ house had _____ windows.

2. The cats licked their fur.
The _____ cats licked their _____ fur.

3. Aunt Sophia stirred the stew with a spoon.
Aunt Sophia stirred the _____ stew with a _____ spoon.

Answers will vary.

78 — Week 6 — Thursday

Page 79

Language Bytes

Number the words in each list in alphabetical order from 1 to 5.

5 termite
1 team
4 tennis
3 ten
2 temper

1 macaroni
2 magazine
5 marigold
4 maple
3 maid

2 different
1 dice
4 divide
5 dishes
3 dim

MATH TIME — Find the answers.

$9R1$ $\quad$ 6 $\quad$ $8R2$ $\quad$ $6R2$ $\quad$ $9R3$ $\quad$ $8R3$
$3)\overline{28}$ $\quad$ $4)\overline{24}$ $\quad$ $5)\overline{42}$ $\quad$ $6)\overline{38}$ $\quad$ $6)\overline{57}$ $\quad$ $9)\overline{75}$

$7R4$ $\quad$ $8R1$ $\quad$ $8R5$ $\quad$ $9R1$ $\quad$ $9R4$ $\quad$ $9R2$
$6)\overline{46}$ $\quad$ $7)\overline{57}$ $\quad$ $8)\overline{69}$ $\quad$ $9)\overline{82}$ $\quad$ $5)\overline{49}$ $\quad$ $3)\overline{29}$

$7R4$ $\quad$ $6R1$ $\quad$ $8R3$ $\quad$ $2R5$ $\quad$ 9 $\quad$ $4R1$
$7)\overline{53}$ $\quad$ $4)\overline{25}$ $\quad$ $8)\overline{67}$ $\quad$ $7)\overline{19}$ $\quad$ $9)\overline{81}$ $\quad$ $7)\overline{29}$

Friday — Week 6 — 79

Page 80

What's wrong with this picture?

There are many things wrong with this park scene.
Find them. Tell someone what you found.

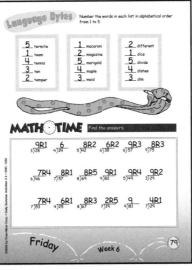

80 — Week 6 — Friday

Page 83

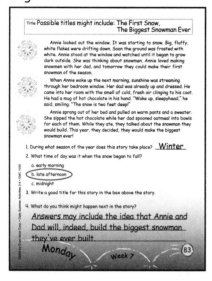

Title: Possible titles might include: The First Snow, The Biggest Snowman Ever

Annie looked out the window. It was starting to snow. Big, fluffy, white flakes were drifting down. Soon the ground was frosted with white. Annie stood at the window and watched until it began to grow dark outside. She was thinking about snowmen. Annie loved making snowmen with her dad, and tomorrow they could make their first snowman of the season.

When Annie woke up the next morning, sunshine was streaming through her bedroom window. Her dad was already up and dressed. He came into her room with the smell of cold, fresh air clinging to his coat. He had a mug of hot chocolate in his hand. "Wake up, sleepyhead," he said, smiling. "The snow is two feet deep!"

Annie sprang out of her bed and pulled on warm pants and a sweater. She sipped the hot chocolate while her dad spooned oatmeal into bowls for each of them. While they ate, they talked about the snowman they would build. This year, they decided, they would make the biggest snowman ever!

1. During what season of the year does this story take place? __Winter__

2. What time of day was it when the snow began to fall?
   a. early morning
   (b.) late afternoon
   c. midnight

3. Write a good title for this story in the box above the story.

4. What do you think might happen next in the story?
__Answers may include the idea that Annie and Dad will, indeed, build the biggest snowman they've ever built.__

Monday   Week 7   83

Page 84

Write It Right

1. father and me eat the pancakes yesterday
__Father and I ate the pancakes yesterday.__

2. uncle sylvester wear a funny costume last halloween
__Uncle Sylvester wore a funny costume last Halloween.__

3. our class we had fun going threw the museum
__Our class had fun going through the museum.__

MATH TIME   Find the answers.

40 ×2 **80**	33 ×1 **33**	52 ×8 **416**	100 ×4 **400**	67 ×2 **134**	35 ×9 **315**	13 ×3 **39**
94 ×2 **188**	28 ×4 **112**	71 ×9 **639**	86 ×6 **516**	18 ×8 **144**	82 ×5 **410**	60 ×7 **420**

84   Week 7   Monday

Page 85

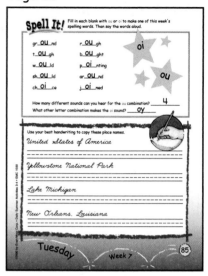

Spell It!

Fill in each blank with ou or oi to make one of this week's spelling words. Then say the words aloud.

gr__ou__nd	r__ou__gh
t__ou__gh	b__ou__ght
w__ou__ld	p__oi__nting
sh__ou__ld	ar__ou__nd
ch__oi__ce	j__oi__ned

How many different sounds can you hear for the ou combination? __4__
What other letter combination makes the oi sound? __oy__

Use your best handwriting to copy these place names.
United States of America
Yellowstone National Park
Lake Michigan
New Orleans, Louisiana

Tuesday   Week 7   85

Page 86

Language Bytes

Adverbs are words that tell how, when, or where things happen. Some adverbs are listed below. Decide whether each word tells how, when, or where and write it under the correct heading.

How	When	Where
softly	sometimes	anywhere
sweetly	early	here
sadly	never	there
bravely	today	everywhere

anywhere sweetly never there
sometimes here today everywhere
softly early sadly bravely

MATH TIME   Find the answers.

4R4 5)24	**6R1** 6)37	**4R2** 8)34	**7R1** 4)29	**9R2** 4)38	**9R4** 9)85
6R6 7)48	**6R4** 9)58	**8R3** 8)67	**8** 8)64	**9R6** 9)78	**6R1** 7)43

86   Week 7   Tuesday

Page 87

The Planet Mars

Mars is the fourth planet in our solar system. It is about 142 million miles away from the Sun. You can often see Mars in the sky. It looks like a bright, reddish star. The red color comes from the red dust on the surface of the planet. This dust is often swirled into the thin atmosphere on Mars by fierce windstorms.

Mars is a fairly small planet. It is about one-half the size of Earth. The North and South Poles of the planet are covered with ice and snow. Mars has volcanoes, mountains, canyons, and craters. There are odd lines and streaks on the surface of Mars that some scientists think may be old riverbeds. Mars has two small moons.

Space vehicles have been sent to Mars to take pictures and collect soil samples. Recently, scientists found evidence that there may have been simple life-forms on Mars at some time in the past. They examined rocks from Mars that seemed to contain the remains of some bacteria. Scientists continue to study and learn more about Mars. Someday, people from Earth may even visit our neighboring planet.

Mark each statement true (T) or false (F).
__F__ Mars is larger than Earth.
__T__ Mars can be seen from Earth.
__T__ Mars is the fourth planet in the solar system.
__T__ The surface of Mars is covered with red dust.
__F__ Scientists think large animals once lived on Mars.
__F__ The surface of Mars is very smooth and flat.
__F__ Mars is a star.

Wednesday   Week 7   87

Page 88

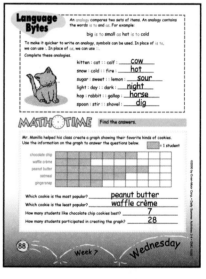

Language Bytes

An analogy compares two sets of items. An analogy contains the words is to and as. For example:
big is to small as hot is to cold

To make it quicker to write an analogy, symbols can be used. In place of to, we can use :. In place of as, we can use ::.

Complete these analogies.

kitten : cat :: calf :	__cow__
snow : cold :: fire :	__hot__
sugar : sweet :: lemon :	__sour__
light : day :: dark :	__night__
hop : rabbit :: gallop :	__horse__
spoon : stir :: shovel :	__dig__

MATH TIME   Find the answers.

Mr. Manilla helped his class create a graph showing their favorite kinds of cookies. Use the information on the graph to answer the questions below.   ▢ = 1 student

chocolate chip								
waffle crème								
peanut butter								
oatmeal								
gingersnap								

Which cookie is the most popular? __peanut butter__
Which cookie is the least popular? __waffle crème__
How many students like chocolate chip cookies best? __7__
How many students participated in creating the graph? __28__

88   Week 7   Wednesday

Page 89

Geography

Maps can give information about the products that are important to a state or a country. This map of Alabama shows some plant and animal products that the state produces.

Alabama

Answer true (T) or false (F).
__F__ Peanuts are grown all over the state.
__T__ Cotton is grown in more areas than corn.
__T__ Animals are raised in most parts of the state.
__T__ Corn is grown in the areas where hogs are raised.
__F__ Twice as many dairy cows as beef cattle are raised.

Legend
hogs   cotton
beef cattle   soybeans
peanuts   poultry
corn   dairy products

In My Own Words

Write a paragraph that describes the animal in the picture.
__Descriptions will vary.__

Thursday   Week 7   89

Page 90

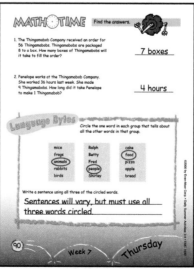

MATH TIME   Find the answers.

1. The Thingamabob Company received an order for 56 Thingamabobs. Thingamabobs are packaged 8 to a box. How many boxes of Thingamabobs will it take to fill the order?
__7 boxes__

2. Penelope works at the Thingamabob Company. She worked 36 hours last week. She made 9 Thingamabobs. How long did it take Penelope to make 1 Thingamabob?
__4 hours__

Language Bytes

Circle the one word in each group that tells about all the other words in that group.

mice	Ralph	cake
frogs	Betty	(food)
(animals)	Fred	pizza
rabbits	(people)	apple
birds	Shirley	bread

Write a sentence using all three of the circled words.
__Sentences will vary, but must use all three words circled.__

90   Week 7   Thursday

Page 91

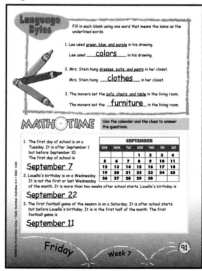

Language Bytes

Fill in each blank using one word that means the same as the underlined words.

1. Lee used green, blue, and purple in his drawing.
Lee used __colors__ in his drawing.

2. Mrs. Stein hung dresses, suits, and pants in her closet.
Mrs. Stein hung __clothes__ in her closet.

3. The movers set the sofa, chairs, and table in the living room.
The movers set the __furniture__ in the living room.

MATH TIME   Use the calendar and the clues to answer the questions.

1. The first day of school is on a Tuesday. It is after September 1 but before September 10. The first day of school is on a
__September 7__

2. Louella's birthday is on a Wednesday. It is not the first or last Wednesday of the month. It is more than two weeks after school starts. Louella's birthday is on
__September 22__

3. The first football game of the season is on a Saturday. It is after school starts but before Louella's birthday. It is in the first half of the month. The first football game is
__September 11__

SEPTEMBER

SUN	MON	TUE	WED	THU	FRI	SAT
	1	2	3	4	5	6
7	8	9	10	11	12	13
14	15	16	17	18	19	20
21	22	23	24	25		
26	27	28	29	30		

Friday   Week 7   91

©2005 by Evan-Moor Corp. • Daily Summer Activities 3-4 • EMC 1030

Page 92

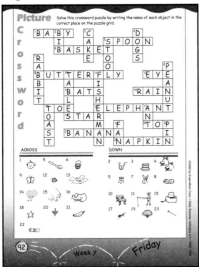

Picture Crossword — Solve this crossword puzzle by writing the name of each object in the correct place on the puzzle grid.

Crossword grid answers:
- BABY, SPOON, DOGS, BASKET, BUTTERFLY, EYE, BATS, RAIN, TOE, ELEPHANT, STAR, TOP, BANANA, NAPKIN

ACROSS / DOWN

Week 7 — Friday

Page 95

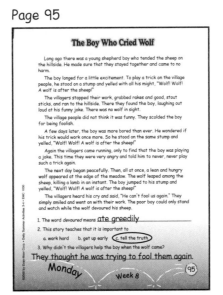

The Boy Who Cried Wolf

Long ago there was a young shepherd boy who tended the sheep on the hillside. He made sure that they stayed together and came to no harm.

The boy longed for a little excitement. To play a trick on the village people, he stood on a stump and yelled with all his might, "Wolf! Wolf! A wolf is after the sheep!"

The villagers stopped their work, grabbed rakes and good, stout sticks, and ran to the hillside. There they found the boy, laughing out loud at his funny joke. There was no wolf in sight.

The village people did not think it was funny. They scolded the boy for being foolish.

A few days later, the boy was more bored than ever. He wondered if his trick would work once more. So he stood on the same stump and yelled, "Wolf! Wolf! A wolf is after the sheep!"

Again the villagers came running, only to find that the boy was playing a joke. This time they were very angry and told him to never, never play such a trick again.

The next day began peacefully. Then, all at once, a lean and hungry wolf appeared at the edge of the meadow. The wolf leaped among the sheep, killing a lamb in an instant. The boy jumped to his stump and yelled, "Wolf! Wolf! A wolf is after the sheep!"

The villagers heard his cry and said, "He can't fool us again." They simply smiled and went on with their work. The poor boy could only stand and watch while the wolf devoured his sheep.

1. The word *devoured* means __ate greedily__

2. This story teaches that it is important to
   a. work hard   b. get up early   (c. tell the truth)

3. Why didn't the villagers help the boy when the wolf came?
__They thought he was trying to fool them again.__

Monday — Week 8

Page 96

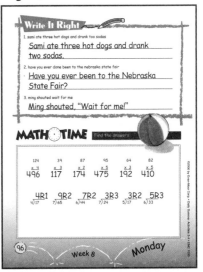

Write It Right

1. sami ate three hot dogs and drank too sodas
__Sami ate three hot dogs and drank two sodas.__

2. have you ever done been to the nebraska state fair
__Have you ever been to the Nebraska State Fair?__

3. ming shouted wait for me
__Ming shouted, "Wait for me!"__

MATH TIME — Find the answers.

124 ×4 = 496	39 ×3 = 117	87 ×2 = 174	95 ×5 = 475	64 ×3 = 192	82 ×5 = 410

4R1 (4)17   9R2 (7)65   7R2 (6)44   3R3 (7)24   3R2 (5)17   5R3 (6)33

Week 8 — Monday

Page 97

Spell It! — Make an X on the silent letter or letters in each of this week's spelling words.

- g**h**ost   clim**b**
- **k**naw   lim**b**
- ri**gh**t   nei**gh**bor
- **k**new   **k**night
- **w**rong   **h**our

Copy this poem using your best handwriting. Find at least three words in the poem that contain silent letters and circle them.

I'd like to live on an island
With the sparkling sea at my door.
I would gather shells in a basket
And write my name on the shore.

Tuesday — Week 8

Page 98

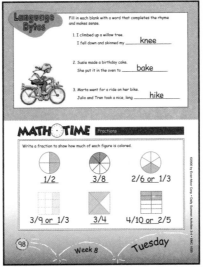

Language Bytes — Fill in each blank with a word that completes the rhyme and makes sense.

1. I climbed up a willow tree.
   I fell down and skinned my __knee__

2. Susie made a birthday cake.
   She put it in the oven to __bake__

3. Marta went for a ride on her bike.
   Julio and Tran took a nice, long __hike__

MATH TIME — Fractions

Write a fraction to show how much of each figure is colored.

1/2   3/8   2/6 or 1/3

3/9 or 1/3   3/4   4/10 or 2/5

Week 8 — Tuesday

Page 99

A Great Civilization

The Aztecs were Native Americans who created a great civilization in the land that is now Mexico. During the 1400s and early 1500s, the Aztecs ruled a powerful empire. They built enormous cities. They made temples, sculptures, and carvings.

Religion was important to the Aztecs. They worshipped many gods and goddesses and held many different kinds of religious ceremonies.

The Aztecs were good farmers. Their main food was corn, which they made into tortillas, or thin, flat pieces of bread. They liked spicy chili peppers in their food. They hunted deer, rabbits, and birds for meat.

Aztec families lived in simple homes made of wood and adobe clay. Everyone in the family, including the children, had to help with chores. These included farming, cooking, weaving cloth, and sewing. Boys went to school for religious and military training. Girls were taught mostly at home.

The Aztec Empire came to an end when Spain invaded it in 1519. The Spanish soldiers destroyed most of the Aztecs' cities and buildings. Fortunately, a few buildings were saved, and many pieces of Aztec artwork are now on display in museums in Mexico City. People today are still fascinated by the Aztecs and their ancient way of life.

1. Who were the Aztecs and where did they live?
__Native Americans who lived in what is now Mexico.__

2. What are some of the things the Aztecs did?
__built large cities, created artworks, farmed, hunted__

3. About how many years ago did the Aztec Empire exist?
(a. 1000)   b. 250   c. 500

4. Why did the Aztec Empire come to an end?
__Spanish soldiers destroyed the empire.__

Wednesday — Week 8

Page 100

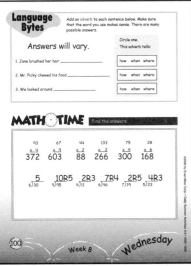

Language Bytes — Add an adverb to each sentence below. Make sure that the word you use makes sense. There are many possible answers.

__Answers will vary.__

Circle one. This adverb tells: how / when / where

1. Jane brushed her hair ____
2. Mr. Picky chewed his food ____
3. We looked around ____

MATH TIME — Find the answers.

93 ×4 = 372	67 ×9 = 603	44 ×2 = 88	133 ×2 = 266	75 ×4 = 300	28 ×6 = 168

5 (6)30   10R5 (9)95   2R3 (4)11   7R4 (6)46   2R5 (7)19   4R3 (5)23

Week 8 — Wednesday

Page 101

Geography

Pierre has found a treasure map. Follow the directions below to help him find the treasure. Make an X on that spot.

Begin at Mystic Mountain.
Go 3 spaces east.
Go 6 spaces north.
Follow the Riddle River 5 spaces east.
Go south 3 spaces and start digging.

In My Own Words

Fill in the blanks in the sentence below. Then write a paragraph using the sentence as a topic sentence.

____ is better than ____

__Writing will vary.__

Thursday — Week 8

Page 102

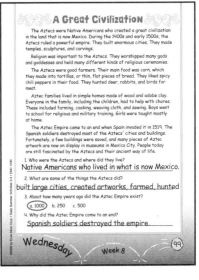

MATH TIME — Match the Money

Count each set of coins and write the amount. Match the coins to the correct person.

- = $1.05 — I have the most money.
- = 75¢ — I have more than 75 cents, but less than a dollar.
- = 82¢ — I have an amount equal to a half-dollar and a quarter.

Language Bytes — Write a homophone to go with each word below. Explain the meanings of all the words to an adult.

- pole — __pail__
- knot — __not__
- blew — __blue__
- dear — __deer__
- rows — __rose__

Week 8 — Thursday

Page 103

Language Bytes
Choose the pronoun that best completes each sentence.

She I He	1. __I__ want to go to the circus tomorrow.
her she their	2. John and Becky almost missed __their__ flight.
he me they	3. Mario visited __me__ at my ranch.
me he they	4. "I am a good baseball player," __he__ said.

MATH TIME — Find the answers.

1. Sandy bought a melon that weighed 3 pounds. It cost 33¢ per pound. How much did she pay for the melon? **99¢**

Sandy paid for the melon with a $5 bill. How much change did she receive? **$4.01**

2. Jim bought some flowers. He bought 2 roses and 4 tulips. The roses cost $2 each. The tulips cost $1.50 each. How much did the flowers cost altogether? **$10.00**

Friday — Week 8 — 103

Page 104

Rebus Puzzle
Add and subtract the letters in the names of the pictures in the order given to find the name of something that would give you a fast ride.

Circle each correct answer.

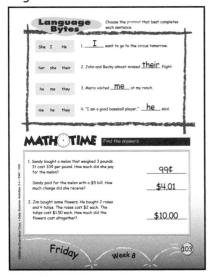

Work area:
star + nlop + lock + egg + tent

Answer: **r o c k e t**

104 — Week 8 — Friday

Page 107

A Busy Trip

The Ryan family took a trip to New York City. First, they walked to the Empire State Building. Next, they took the ferry to the Statue of Liberty. After that, they rode the subway to Central Park. They ate lunch in the park and fed the pigeons. They bought ice-cream cones and then walked by the lake. Late in the afternoon, they took a taxi back to their hotel. After they had dinner, they went to a musical play.

Circle each correct answer.

Did the Ryans eat lunch before or after they saw the Statue of Liberty? before (after)

Did they take a taxi before or after they rode on the ferry? before (after)

Did they feed the pigeons before or after they rode the subway? (before) after

Did they have dinner before or after they went to a musical play? (before) after

Did they see the Empire State Building before or after they went to Central Park? (before) after

Did they buy ice-cream cones before or after they walked by the lake? (before) after

List all the ways the Ryans traveled while in New York City.

on foot/walked, ferry, subway, taxi

Monday — Week 9 — 107

Page 108

Write It Right

1. my brother and me visited our aunt uncle and cousins in chicago
My brother and I visited our aunt, uncle, and cousins in Chicago.

2. do you got a lot of home work tonight
Do you have a lot of homework tonight?

3. we new how to spell all the words on fridays test
We knew how to spell all the words on Friday's test.

MATH TIME — Find the answers.

| 61 +28 = **89** | 73 -46 = **27** | 92 +37 = **129** | 10 +84 = **94** | 54 -16 = **38** | 88 -59 = **29** |

| $1.19 -.65 = **$.54** | $1.22 -.96 = **$.26** | $5.50 +2.30 = **$7.80** | $14.40 +.77 = **$15.17** | $15.60 -6.90 = **$8.70** | $4.70 +6.50 = **$11.20** |

108 — Week 9 — Monday

Page 109

Spell It!
Fill in each blank using the correct form of the word.

long	Jim ran for a __longer__ distance than Randy.
stir	Grandpa __stirred__ his famous barbecue sauce.
study	The girls __studied__ for their tests last night.
swim	We were __swimming__ in the lake when it began to rain.

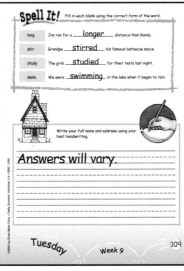

Write your full name and address using your best handwriting.

Answers will vary.

Tuesday — Week 9 — 109

Page 110

Language Bytes
Add adjectives to each sentence below. Make sure that the words you use make sense. There are many possible answers.

1. The elephant stood in the water. **Answers will vary.**
The _____ elephant stood in the _____ water.

2. Dr. Samson sat in a chair and read a book.
Dr. Samson sat in the _____ chair and read the _____ book.

3. The ladies made quilts.
The _____ ladies made _____ quilts.

Now think of additional adjectives that could be used for each sentence.

MATH TIME — Color the correct number of items to show each fraction.

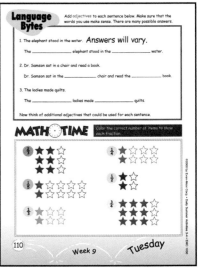

110 — Week 9 — Tuesday

Page 111

?? Another Unnamed Story ??

Veterinarians are animal doctors. They go to school for many years. They learn all kinds of things about animals. They learn what foods animals need for good health. They learn about animal diseases and how to treat and prevent them.

Pet owners depend on veterinarians to help keep their pets healthy. Dogs and cats need regular vaccinations and checkups. They need the right kind of food. They need regular exercise. And pets need love and attention. Veterinarians enjoy working with pet owners to make sure their pets have proper care. Veterinarians also take care of injured animals. They set broken bones, stitch up wounds, and perform surgeries of all kinds.

Some veterinarians do not work with cats and dogs. They specialize in large animals. They work with cows, horses, pigs, and sheep. Other veterinarians are experts in the care of reptiles or birds. Some veterinarians even work at zoos.

Being a veterinarian is a difficult job. It requires a great deal of patience, hard work, and skill. Someone who loves animals can find it to be a very rewarding job.

1. List at least three things that pets need to stay healthy and happy.
regular vaccinations and checkups; the right kind and amount of food; regular exercise; love and attention

2. A good title for this story would be
a. How to Care for Your Pet (b. Animal Doctors) c. Working with Animals

3. What does expert mean?
a person who knows a lot about something

Wednesday — Week 9 — 111

Page 112

Language Bytes
Look up the words below in a dictionary. Read the definition of each word. Then draw a picture to illustrate each definition.

| jetty | scroll |
| Illustration must show a structure built out into the water. | Illustration must show a strip of paper, either open or rolled. |

MATH TIME — Fill in each blank using one of the numbers in the box. Use each number only once.

2 3 4 5

40 x **3** is between 100 and 150.

90 x **2** is between 150 and 200.

65 x **4** is between 200 and 300.

72 x **5** is between 300 and 400.

112 — Week 9 — Wednesday

Page 113

Geography
Draw a map of your house or apartment. Imagine that you have removed the roof and are flying overhead, looking down. Label each room.

Drawings will vary.

In My Own Words
Which room in your house do you like best? Write a paragraph describing that room. Be sure to include details about the things that make that room a special place.
Answers will vary.

Thursday — Week 9 — 113

Page 114

MATH TIME — Use the numbers on each shape to create a multiplication problem.

3 6 / 8 4	1 2 / 5 3	2 / 3 6 9

4 3 or 34
× 2
8 6 or 68

1 3
× 4
5 2

2 3 or 32
× 3
6 9 or 96

Language Bytes — Fill in the blanks using verbs in the past tense. Make sure that the words you choose make sense.

Answers will vary; possibilities include:

1. Yesterday, I _went/drove_ to town to buy a gift for my friend.
2. He _ate/cooked_ nine pancakes for breakfast this morning.
3. The baby goats _slept_ peacefully all night.
4. We _watched_ television for an hour before we went to bed.

114 — Week 9 — Thursday

Page 115

Language Bytes — Combine each pair of sentences to make one sentence.

1. Barbara went to the meeting. I went to the meeting.
   Barbara and I went to the meeting.

2. Ken likes strawberries. Angie likes watermelon.
   Ken likes strawberries, but Angie likes watermelon.

3. Put on your shoes. Put on your jacket.
   Put on your shoes and jacket.

MATH TIME — Complete each drawing. Each finished drawing should be symmetrical.

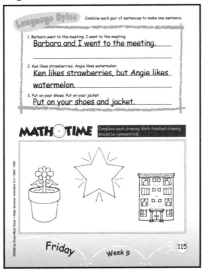

Friday — Week 9 — 115

Page 116

A Hidden Picture

In the scene below, find the following hidden pictures:
ice-cream cone, sock, ring, crown, toothbrush, fish, hand, umbrella, ball, cup, and lamp.

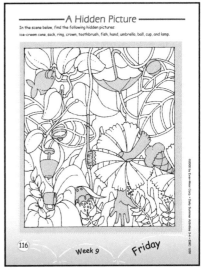

116 — Week 9 — Friday

Page 119

Questions and Answers

Write a question to go with each answer.

Question: What does he like on his hamburger?
Answer: He likes his hamburger with ketchup, pickles, and tomatoes.

Question: How old is she?
Answer: She is eleven years old.

Question: When is the school fair?
Answer: The school fair will be held on the first Saturday in October.

Question: How much money does Natasha have?
Answer: Natasha has eleven dollars.

Question: What did Rupert eat?
Answer: Rupert had a peanut butter and jelly sandwich and an apple.

Question: What did the bugs do when they got to camp?
Answer: The boys set up their tents, took a hike, and cooked dinner.

Now write your own question and answer it.

Question: Answers will vary.
Answer:

Monday — Week 10 — 119

Page 120

Write It Right!

1. wear your read dress to the mozart concert said mother
   "Wear your red dress to the Mozart concert," said Mother.

2. ive got an older brother and a younger sister
   I have an older brother and a younger sister.

3. when you get home tell mike i have went to florida
   When you get home, tell Mike I have gone to Florida.

MATH TIME — Find the answers.

329	211	136	199	287	306
−146	−54	+242	−98	−129	−142
183	157	378	101	158	164

185	257	340	175	127	169
+216	+169	−270	+84	+127	+352
401	426	70	259	254	521

120 — Week 10 — Monday

Page 121

Spell It! — Write a word that means the opposite of each word below.

fastest	slowest
beautiful	ugly, unattractive
strongest	weakest
careful	careless
happiest	saddest

Write this sentence using your best handwriting.

Jake opened the gigantic yellow box and found a marvelous quetzal inside.

What is a quetzal? Use a dictionary or an encyclopedia to find out. Draw a picture of a quetzal.

Picture should show a brightly colored bird with a long tail.

Tuesday — Week 10 — 121

Page 122

Language Bytes — If the guide words on a dictionary page were *hair* and *hamper*, which of the following words would *not* appear on that page? Cross off each word that would not appear.

hair		hamper

half   ~~habit~~
~~handle~~   hammer
halo   hall
~~haunt~~   halibut
hale   ~~hay~~

MATH TIME — Use a ruler to measure each object.

Measure to the nearest half inch.

$2\frac{1}{2}$ inches

3 inches

2 inches

$4\frac{1}{2}$ inches

122 — Week 10 — Tuesday

Page 123

How to Bake a Cake

Below are directions for baking a cake, but they are all mixed up! Number the sentences from 1 to 9 to put the directions in the order that makes sense. Draw a line through the one sentence that does *not* belong with the others.

5 Pour the batter into the cake pans.
4 Mix the ingredients together according to the recipe.
8 Allow the cake to cool.
9 Spread frosting over the top and sides of the cake.
1 Wash your hands.
~~Chop two large onions.~~
2 Read the recipe to make sure you have all the ingredients.
6 Place the cake in the oven to bake.
7 Remove the cake from the oven.
3 Measure all ingredients carefully.

What is your favorite kind of cake?
Answers will vary.

Wednesday — Week 10 — 123

Page 124

Language Bytes — Complete each sentence using an adjective and an adverb. Make sure that the words you use make sense. There are many possible answers.

Answers will vary.

1. The bear walked into the woods.
   The _____ bear walked _____ into the woods.

2. The girl wrapped the package.
   The _____ girl _____ wrapped the package.

3. The teacher spoke to the class.
   The _____ teacher spoke _____ to the class.

MATH TIME — Find the answers.

1. Rudy has a pizza parlor. On Friday he sold 114 pepperoni pizzas, 98 cheese pizzas, and 49 mushroom pizzas. How many pizzas did he sell on Friday?
   261 pizzas

2. On Saturday Rudy sold 22 more pepperoni pizzas than he did on Friday. He also sold 62 mushroom pizzas and 97 cheese pizzas. How many pepperoni pizzas did he sell on Saturday?
   136 pepperoni pizzas

3. How many pizzas did Rudy sell on Friday and Saturday together?
   556 pizzas

124 — Week 10 — Wednesday

Page 125

Geography

Draw a map showing how to get from your home to a place you can walk to. This might be a friend's house, a park, or a store. Label each street.

Drawings will vary.

In My Own Words

Make a list of at least five words that can be used in place of the word *said*. Use three of the words in a sentence.

Answers will vary, but may include:

declared	answered	shouted
stated	reported	muttered
responded	uttered	stammered
replied	whispered	cried

Thursday — Week 10 — 125

Page 126

MATH TIME — Find the answers.

321	65	135	25	100	71
642	390	675	75	3000	426

246	19	159	280	76	200
492	57	477	560	304	8000

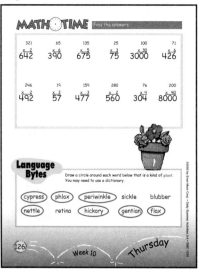

Language Bytes

Draw a circle around each word below that is a kind of plant. You may need to use a dictionary.

(cypress) (phlox) (periwinkle) sickle blubber
(nettle) retina (hickory) (gentian) (flax)

126 — Week 10 — Thursday

Page 127

Language Bytes

Fill in each blank using a group of words that gives more information about the underlined word.

Answers will vary.

1. Our family has <u>pets</u>.
   Our family has three large dogs and a cat

2. Lenny keeps his <u>toys</u> on the shelf.
   Lenny keeps his Hot Wheels and his ball on the shelf.

3. Anna plays several <u>sports</u>.
   Anna plays soccer, T-ball, field hockey

MATH TIME — Find the answers.

This graph shows the number of students in each grade at Topanga Elementary School. Use the information on the graph to answer the questions.

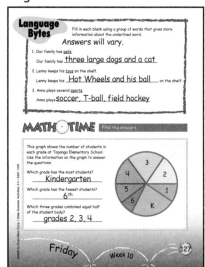

Which grade has the most students?
Kindergarten

Which grade has the fewest students?
6th

Which three grades combined equal half of the student body?
grades 2, 3, 4

Friday — Week 10 — 127

Page 128

Australian Friend

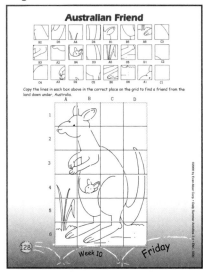

Copy the lines in each box above in the correct place on the grid to find a friend from the land down under, Australia.

128 — Week 10 — Friday

©2005 by Evan-Moor Corp. • Daily Summer Activities 3–4 • EMC 1030

Spell It!

This list contains all of the spelling words for weeks 1 through 10.

afraid	close	group	piece	swimming
age	clothes	happiest	playing	they
almost	coast	having	please	thoughtless
aren't	cube	homework	pointing	throne
around	didn't	hour	prey	tiny
away	doesn't	I'll	quietly	tough
basketball	don't	joined	raise	turned
beautiful	eight	joked	received	useful
become	everybody	knew	right	usually
blew	fastest	knight	rough	weight
bought	fearless	know	sew	we're
break	field	let's	should	while
butterfly	finally	limb	silent	whole
can't	fuel	longer	smarter	without
careful	funniest	maybe	smiling	wonderful
chew	future	menu	something	won't
choice	ghost	music	spelling	would
choose	gnaw	myself	stirred	wouldn't
clean	great	neighbor	strongest	wrong
climb	ground	outside	studied	wrote